All about GROUND COVERS

Basic text and research by
Don Dimond
Michael MacCaskey

Edited and coordinated by
Scott Millard

Designed by
Craig Bergquist

Photography by
William Aplin
Michael Landis

Special consultant
Sara Godwin

Contents

They cover the ground

**Ground covers are the practical plants of the landscape — the problem solvers.
They are used to accent, blend, and unify the other elements of the home garden.
But when viewed with an imaginative eye, they do much more than just cover the ground.**

Imagine a tree-shaded bed of pachysandra, or a cool carpet of heart-shaped violets bordering a walkway. Picture a steep slope blanketed in steel-blue juniper or bright green Algerian ivy. Envision the gentle colors and textures created by a bed of mondo grass blending into a lawn. These are just a few of the uses of the versatile plants known as ground covers — plants that creep, clump, mat, and vine to cover, conceal, and protect the bare soil. They can be deciduous or evergreen, broadleaved or needleleaved, ranging in size from plants a few inches high to shrubs that reach three or more feet. Whether low-growing perennials, deciduous shrubs, or sprawling vines, they are valued for their ability to spread rapidly, stay close to the ground, and create a thick, low-maintenance covering that binds and holds the soil. Ground covers are, simply, plants that cover the ground. Creeping plants such as bird's foot ivy spread over the ground like a mat; cotoneaster and juniper depend on the interlacing of leaves and branches to create a living carpet.

Ground covers could be described as the most underrated plants in the landscape, but they are the most versatile, and in some situations, the most valuable landscape plants. Seldom taking center stage, they more often provide "back-up support" for other plants, integrating and completing a landscape scheme.

Ground covers create interest in an oft-neglected area — the earth's floor. They add texture and color on a new

◁

A trailing bed of creeping Jenny (Lysimachia nummularia) covers and protects this steep, rocky slope in a colorful way.

scale. Just as you choose your carpeting to enhance your home furnishings, you can choose ground covers to complement your landscape and architecture.

The importance of perspective

Choosing the right ground cover for your home depends on *scale.* A ground cover three feet high might be suitable beneath a tall building, but out of place around a small house. Another might be suitable on an open plain but look cramped in a fenced yard. In order to obtain the desired balanced effect, proportion must be kept in mind when selecting a ground cover. In this book we are mostly concerned with low-growing plants up to 18"; the smaller the plant, the more versatile it is as a ground cover. Plants that travel in a horizontal direction offer a challenging array of possibilities, both common and creative.

Valuable and versatile

Ground covers fill a wide variety of needs in the garden. They can be substituted for lawns where grasses will not thrive because of steep slopes, poor soil, dense shade, or exposed tree roots. They can be used to cover areas of barren soil, to highlight other plants, and to create interest in every inch of your garden. They can even be used to cover stone walls or to drape from window boxes.

Ground covers are very diverse. Whether there is deep shade or poor soil or limited moisture, a ground cover can be found to suit the site. In thickly wooded yards where little light penetrates to the ground, plants native to the forest floor are useful ground covers. Plants for this environment are periwinkle, winter-creeper, or goutweed. There are other plants that require little water; in fact, that's how they grow best. Cotoneaster, juniper, and ivy are all drought

A planting of mondo grass blends with lawn to create a relaxing, unified landscape. Note the ivy-shrouded trees in background.

resistant. There is a ground cover to suit any soil type: sand, clay, acid, alkaline, moist ,or dry. Every plant has a soil type to which it is best adapted. Most of the herbs, such as dwarf rosemary or creeping thyme, will do well in poor soil. By choosing the right plant for your soil you can insure a thick, healthy ground cover.

As a landscape harmonizer

If you need to emphasize the patterns and unify the elements of your garden, there's a ground cover to do the job. They bring a continuity of coverage to all areas, creating a feeling of tranquility. In addition to setting off other plants and highlighting the shaded areas under shrubs and trees, ground covers protect the soil by preventing erosion and act as the most attractive sort of mulch by keeping the soil cool and moist.

Although a solid-massed effect is the intention of ground covers, some plants become too prolific and may eventually invade flower beds or grassy areas. A simple barrier such as a two-by-four border or brick edging will contain them. Pruning will also control rampant growers.

Keeping a low profile

Some of the more unusual ground covers are the small-leaved plants that work so well in the odd little nooks and crannies of a yard. They creep into hard-to-reach places and are often so small they are best appreciated on hands and knees or belly down. Cool baby's-tears, or sweet-smelling lemon thyme will grow in the cracks of a brick walk, in a back corner, in the pockets of a rock, or under a rainspout. Delicate in appear-

Bands of sweet alyssum and Scotch and Irish moss add a pleasing color and texture contrast to rough-hewn wooden timbers.

ance, they are generally hardy and require little care. Both are especially effective between stepping stones or anywhere that low coverage is needed. Scarcely three inches high, they soften the edges of bricks or stonework and blend garden paths smoothly into the rest of the garden. They tolerate heavy moisture and little light; their matting habit prevents splashing and run-off during rain which aids in water absorption.

Problem solvers

Ground covers can be used to cover a large area or just the difficult-to-mow space at the base of a tree. A thick ground cover can reduce the maintenance under dirty trees because the litter from leaves, flowers, fruit, or bark quietly vanishes into and beneath the ground cover. The litter eventually breaks down and enriches the soil, to the benefit of both the tree and the ground cover.

Ground covers prevent erosion on steep slopes where maintenance would be difficult. They can create borders along walks or fill in an area where other plants would be hard to maintain. Some ground covers can be used as barriers, and for directing foot traffic. There are also tall-growing or vining ground covers that are useful for covering rocks or hiding unsightly spots. Some planting areas, such as freeway banks, are difficult and even dangerous to maintain.

A low mass of violet ground cover helps soften the lines of a brick walk, and provides the finishing touch to a layered landscape look.

A bed of hosta solves the problem of mowing around the base of a ginkgo tree.

It's in areas like these that the ground cover workhorses — the ivies, junipers, honeysuckle, and vincas really shine. They create carpets of soft green while they control erosion. They cover quickly and do not require frequent watering or maintenance.

Choosing a ground cover

Selection of a ground cover, the area in which it is to be used, and the method of planting vary from region to region. Ground covers are often used in areas where growing conditions are difficult—poor soil, high wind exposure, full sun, or dense shade— but they should also be considered for areas with good growing conditions because of their beauty and attractive flowers. The brilliant bloom of many ground covers adds a special bonus to their ornamental value. Some ground cover plantings provide uniform mass of foliage color throughout the year (juniper), others provide color only from spring to fall (hosta). The herbal ground covers have fragrant foliage as well.

As a landscape accent

Ground covers can serve to highlight or accent the other plants in your garden. They provide variety in height, texture, and color, often making a more exciting contribution to a yard than grass. Ground covers used in combinations create variety in depth and texture. The glossy leaves of ivy combine well with the soft blue-gray matte effect of juniper. Try planting daffodils or other bulbs in ivy; the flowers show up dramatically against ivy's bright green foliage. Later, the ivy will help conceal the dying leaves of the bulbs. Inter-

Ground covers take to creativity: Scotch moss integrates with weathered wood.

Purple plumes of ajuga and Vinca minor *(far right) guide strollers down path.*

planting annuals with your newly planted ground cover will improve appearances immensely while your ground cover is getting established, and the annuals will have died back by the time the ground cover needs the space.

Cooking with ground covers

Many herbs slip smoothly into the role of ground covers. They grow almost anywhere and don't require the best of anything to grow rampant. Just sunlight and benevolent neglect are all they need to be handsome — and in the best of taste. Some herbs can become weedy under good

garden conditions, but shearing will keep them nicely under control. Yard and cooking are improved in one simple snip. If planted just outside the kitchen door herbs are handy for the cook to harvest. A dooryard corner a foot square will grow most of the commonly used herbs — parsley, marjoram, thyme, and rosemary — in sufficient quantity for a family of four. If your dooryard is a fire escape or a small balcony, grow a herb garden in a strawberry jar. The creeping habit that makes herbs a star as ground covers, makes them tumble and fall in fragrant profusion from the pockets of the jar. Where winters are severe, many herbs will thrive indoors with bright light.

Ivy is one ground cover that is at home growing over banks and rolling hills. Here, the addition of junipers bordering the sidewalk adds a color and texture contrast.

Many herbs will tolerate poor soil, full sun, little water, even sandy, sea-side conditions. Brushing your hand across them releases the rich perfume of their foliage, a delicious experience even if the herbs never make it into a bubbling pot of spaghetti sauce. And the clean fragrance of herbs after a good rain could be described as the very definition of freshness.

Old-fashioned names

For the gardener who wants a touch of the old-fashioned, there are ground covers with unusual intriguing names to pique curiosity—madwort (*Alyssum saxatile*), lamb's ears (*Stachys byzantina*), bleeding-heart (*Dicentra spectabilis*), or creeping Jenny (*Lysimachia nummularia*). Some are furry and nice to touch, like lamb's ears, some were used medicinally in ancient times, like madwort. Some ground covers are soft and cool, like baby's-tears and Irish moss. These make excellent underplantings, as a living mulch beneath trees and shrubs, or to cover the exposed soil in a pot. Try Irish moss under azaleas, or baby's-tears creeping over the edge of a pot containing a miniature rose. Or use Scotch moss to give a finished look to bonsai.

Requiring an imaginative mind

Ground covers are versatile, and need to be looked at imaginatively. Wandering Jew can be a ground cover in mild climates, or a house plant anywhere. Juniper can control erosion on a slope, be a bonsai, or make a dramatic hanging-basket subject. Instead of grass, try the small yellow flowers and dark green foliage of *Potentilla verna* for your front lawn. For foliage color, the lusty hue of bronze ajuga will fill an odd spot in the garden ,or spread over a large expanse. *Festuca ovina 'glauca'* with its geometric mounds will produce an unusual border, or create a striking pattern in a street-side parkway. Honeysuckle works as a thick fragrant ground cover or drapes magnificently from a window box. Focus attention on a handsomely shaped cotoneaster by giving it center stage in a con-tainer, or let *Santolina chamaecy-parissus* drape its small, pin-cushion flowers over a planter for a dramatic effect.

Take a close look

Have fun with ground covers — look at them close-up and admire the variations in their texture, form, and structure. Notice the delicate coloration of dusty-miller, *(Artemesia stelleriana)* the bright violet flowers of campanula, the texture of the serrated leaves of *Pachysandra procumbens.* Look at the adhesive discs on ivy, the bright red berries of cotoneaster, and the overlapping scales of juniper.

For a carpet of green, a mass of color, a mound of fragrance, ground covers are the answer. Ground covers satisfy almost every sense—touch, taste, smell, sight — and some of them cover so fast you can almost hear them growing. This book will help you find a ground cover that will spread across that bare slope, fill that quiet, shaded corner, or drape over that empty container.

A front lawn doesn't have to be planted in grass. Potentilla verna *is a colorful, low-maintenance alternative.*

Mounding pattern of Festuca ovina *'glauca' is striking addition to landscape.*

The rustic, enduring qualities of juniper are best appreciated close-up.

Like miniature trumpets, a grouping of Campanula 'Canterbury Bells' thrusts its delicate blossoms skyward. Excellent as a hanging basket subject.

The multicolored foliage of bronze ajuga, shown here bordering lawn as an accent plant, will also spread to cover a large area.

Red on red: cotoneaster berries drape over the subtle earth-red of a brick wall.

Which ground cover?

The following chapter is designed to make it easier to match a ground cover to a site, or a site to a ground cover. In any case, we hope it will simplify the selection process.

Here begins an encyclopedic listing of plants useful as ground covers. Within these pages you can find a plant for virtually every kind of garden as well as for nearly every kind of gardener.

Our descriptive list of ground-covering plants is extensive, including plants for rock gardens, hardy perennials, and even plants normally considered useful only as shrubs. An effort was made to write the plant descriptions in clear, understandable language; we hope you don't have to reach for your dictionary too often. The descriptions are based on the plant's distinguishing features, and the best way to grow and propagate them. Understand that, in most respects, plants are not completely predictable so statements such as "fast growing" or "drought tolerant" are relative terms. A plant that grows as an unmanageable weed in one location could be quite well behaved in another.

Understanding names

Which ground cover? is alphabetical by botanical names. A plant may be known by several common names, but each plant has only one "botanical handle," and it remains the same around the world. Botanical names (as used in this book) are made up of these parts.

The genus name. A genus is a group of plants that are similar in many botanical characteristics. The genus name is the first word of a plant's name. For example, the genus

◁
Nursery shopping: fun and difficult at the same time. Doing your gardening homework will make selecting a ground cover easier.

name of the junipers, *Juniperus.*

The species name. This is the second word of a plant's name. A species is defined as a plant with characteristics that distinguish it from other plants in the same genus and are consistent from generation to generation. An example is *Juniperus chinensis,* the Chinese juniper.

The variety name. Some plants in this encyclopedia have a third name — the variety. Varieties have slight differences from the species and occur in the wild. An example is the sargent juniper, *Juniperus chinensis sargentii.*

The selection name. These are the many plants that are maintained in cultivation because of specific desirable traits. Usually they must be propagated vegetatively. This name is capitalized and between single quotation marks. An example is the juniper 'Blue Pacific.'

We would like to be able to simplify the plant classification by using only common names, but because there are so many, even for the same plant, an encyclopedia of this sort would tend to confuse instead of help. As we mentioned previously, the ground covers in this chapter are listed alphabetically by botanical name. If you don't know or can't remember a plant's botanical name, we've included a reference list of common names along with their botanical counterparts on page 10.

Understanding photographs

You'll notice several photo spreads throughout this chapter. We felt the ground covers featured on these pages were so important to the homeowner they deserved their own photo

session. The descriptions of these plants are listed alphabetically in the chapter.

Group effort

We've had a lot of help in preparing and organizing this section of the book. Many authors, researchers, and growers from many climates throughout the United States and Canada have contributed their opinions, observations, and experience. By no means do we consider this list complete, but not even the most enthusiastic grower of ground covers could grow all of the plants listed here. Our list may be long but every gardener knows plants are ever-changing, ever-adapting, and are constantly being changed and adapted by man. There will always be more plants that grow to cover the ground.

Ground cover display at Arnold Arboretum, Case Estates, Weston, Mass.

Index of common names

Common name	Botanical name
A	
Aaron's beard	Hypericum calycinum
Alpine bugle	Ajuga genevensis
Alpine cinquefoil	Potentilla cinerea
Alpine rock-cress	Arabis alpina
American barrenwort	Vancouveria hexandra
Angel's hair	Artemisia
Andorra juniper	Juniperus horizontalis 'Plumosa'
Australian violet	Viola hederacea
B	
Baby wintercreeper	Euonymus 'Minima'
Barren strawberry	Waldensteinia fragarioides
Barrenwort	Epimedium
Basket-of-gold	Alyssum saxatile
Bearberry	Arctostaphylos uva-ursi
Bearberry cotoneaster	Cotoneaster dammeri
Bellflower	Campanula
Bishop's hat	Epimedium
Bishop's weed	Aegopodium podagraria
Blue fescue	Festuca ovina 'glauca'
Blunt plantain lily	Hosta decorata
Bog rosemary	Andromeda polifolia
Boston ivy	Parthenocissus tricuspidata
British Columbia wild ginger	Asarum caudatum
Broom	Cytisus
Bugleweed	Ajuga
Bunchberry	Cornus canadensis
Burro's-tail	Sedum morganianum
C	
Canadian wild ginger	Asarum canadense
Canby	Paxistima (Pachistima)
Carpet bugle	Ajuga reptans
Catmint	Nepeta mussinii
Catnip	Nepeta cataria
Chamomile	Chamaemelum nobile (Anthemis nobilis)
Checkerberry	Gaultheria
Christmas fern	Polystichum acrostichoides
Christmas heath	Erica carnea
Cinquefoil	Potentilla
Cliff-green	Paxistima (Pachistima)
Coastal wood fern	Dryopteris arguta
Common aubrieta	Aubrieta deltoides
Confederate violet	Viola priceana
Coralbells	Heuchera sanguinea
Corsican mint	Mentha requienii
Cottage pink	Dianthus plumarius
Cranberry cotoneaster	Cotoneaster apiculatus
Creeping cotoneaster	Cotoneaster adpressus
Creeping Jenny	Lysimachia
Creeping juniper	Juniperus horizontalis
Creeping lilyturf	Liriope spicata
Creeping mahonia	Mahonia repens
Creeping Norway spruce	Picea abies 'Repens'
Creeping speedwell	Veronica repens
Creeping thyme	Thymus serpyllum
Crested iris	Iris cristata
Crown vetch	Coronilla varia
Cytisus	Cytisus
D	
Daylily	Hemerocallis
Donkey's-tail	Sedum morganianum
Dusty-miller	Artemisia

Common name	Botanical name
Dwarf deodar cedar	Cedrus deodara 'Repandans'
Dwarf germander	Teucrium chamaedrys 'Prostratum'
Dwarf highbush cranberry	Viburnum opulus 'Nanum'
Dwarf Japanese fleece-flower	P. cuspidatum 'compactum'
Dwarf Japanese garden juniper	Juniperus chinensis procumbens 'Nana'
E	
English ivy	Hedera helix 'Hibernica'
English lavender	Lavandula angustifolia
English yew (spreading)	Taxus baccata 'Repandens'
European wild ginger	Asarum europeaum
Evergreen candytuft	Iberis sempervirens
F	
False spirea	Astilbe
Feverfew	Chrysanthemum parthenium
Five-finger fern	Adiantum
Five-leaf akebia	Akebia quinata
Fleeceflower	Polygonum
Florist's fern	Dryopteris austriaca 'spinulosa'
Foamflower	Tiarella
Fragrant plantain lily	Hosta plantaginea
Fringed bleeding-heart	Dicentra eximia
Funkia	Hosta
G	
Geneva bugle	Ajuga
Germander	Teucrium chamaedrys
Gill-over-the-ground	Glechoma hederacea
Gold-dust	Alyssum saxatile
Gold-moss stonecup	Sedum acre
Goutweed	Aegopodium podagraria
Grass pink	Dianthus plumarius
Green carpet	Herniaria glabra
Ground ivy	Glechoma hederacea
H	
Hall's honeysuckle	Lonicera japonica 'Halliana'
Heartleaf bergenia	Bergenia cordifolia
Heath	Erica
Heather	Calluna vulgaris
Hen-and-chickens	Sempervivum tectorum
Himalayan cotoneaster	Cotoneaster congestus
Himalayan fleeceflower	Polygonum affine
Holly	Ilex
Honeysuckle	Lonicera
Hungarian speedwell	Veronica latifolia 'prostrata'
I	
Indian strawberry	Duchesnea
Irish moss	Sagina subulata
Ivy	Hedera
J	
Japanese barberry	Berberis thunbergii
Japanese ivy	Hedera rhombea
Japanese painted fern	Athyrium georingianum 'pictum'
Japanese spurge	Pachysandra terminalis
Juniper	Juniperus

Common name	Botanical name
K	
Kew wintercreeper	Euonymus fortunei 'Kewensis'
Kinnikinnick	Arctostaphylos
Knotweed	Polygonum
L	
Lady fern	Athyrium filix-femina
Lamb's-ears	Stachys byzantina (Stachys olympica)
Lavender cotton	Santolina chamaecyparissus
Leatherwood fern	Dryopteris marginalis
Lemon thyme	Thymus x citriodorus
Lily-of-the-Nile	Agapanthus
Lily-of-the-valley	Convallaria majalis
Lilyturf	Liriope
Lingonberry	Vaccinium
Lippia	Lippia canescens
Lobularia	Lobularia
M	
Madwort	Alyssum
Maidenhair fern	Adiantum pedatum
Maiden pink	Dianthus deltoides
Manzanita	Arctostaphylos
Mazus	Mazus reptans
Meadowsweet	Astilbe
Memorial rose	Rosa wichuraiana
Mock strawberry	Duchesnea
Mondo grass	Ophiopogon japonicus
Moneywort	Lysimachia nummularia
Moss phlox	Phlox subulata
Moss sandwort	Arenaria
Mossy stonecrop	Sedum acre
Mountain-lover	Paxistima (Pachistima)
Mountain rock cress	Arabis alpina
Mother-of-thyme	Thymus serpyllum
Mugho pine	Pinus mugo 'mughus'
Myrtle	Vinca minor
N	
Narrow-leaved plantain lily	Hosta lancifolia
Necklace cotoneaster	Cotoneaster conspicuus 'decorus'
Nepal ivy	Hedera nepalensis
Norway spruce	Picea abies
O	
Oregon boxwood	Paxistima myrsinites
Oregon grape	Mahonia aquitolium
P	
Pearlwort	Sagina sublata
Periwinkle	Vinca
Pernettya	Pernettya mucronata
Persian ivy	Hedera colchica
Pink creeping thyme	Thymus serpyllum 'Roseus'
Pinks	Dianthus
Plantain lilies	Hostas
Pork and beans	Sedum quaternalense (x rubrotinctum)
Prostrate rosemary	Rosmarinus officinalis 'Prostratus'
Purpleleaf wintercreeper	Euonymus fortunei 'Colorata'
Pyrenees cotoneaster	Cotoneaster congestus
R	
Red-osier dogwood	Cornus sericea
Ribbon grass	Phalaris arundinacea 'picta'
Rock cress	Arabis
Rockspray cotoneaster	Cotoneaster microphylla
Rose	Rosa
Rupturewort	Herniaria glabra

Common name	Botanical name
S	
Salal	Gaultheria shallon 'San Jose'
Sand strawberry	Fragaria chiloensis
Sandy pink	Dianthus arenarius
San Jose juniper	Juniperus chinensis
Savin juniper	Juniperus sabina
Scotch heather	Calluna vulgaris
Scotch moss	Sagina subulata 'Aurea'
Scotch pink	Dianthus plumarius
Sea pink	Armeria maritima
Serbian bellflower	Campanula poscharskyana
Shield ferns	Polystichum
Shore juniper	Juniperus conferta
Siberian tea	Bergenia crassifolia
Small Himalayan sarcococca	Sarcococca hookeriana 'humilis'
Small-leaved cotoneaster	Cotoneaster microphyllus
Snow-in-summer	Cerastium tomentosum
Speedwell	Veronica
Spotted dead nettle	Lamium
Spring cinquefoil	Potentilla verna
Spring heath	Erica carnea maculatum
St.-John's-wort	Hypericum calycinum
Stonecrop	Sedum
Sweet alyssum	Lobularia maritima
Sweet woodruff	Galium odoratum
T	
Thrift	Armeria maritima
Thyme	Thymus
V	
Variegated goutweed	Aegopodium podagraria 'Variegatum'
Variegated wintercreeper	Euonymus fortunei 'Gracilis'
Violet	Viola
Virginia creeper	Parthenocissus quinquefolia
W	
Wall rock cress	Arabis caucasica
Wavy-leaved plantain lily	Hosta undulata
Western sword fern	Polystichum munitum
Whisky nose	Sedum guatemalense (x rubrotinctum)
White Chinese indigo	Indigofera incarnata 'Alba'
White creeping thyme	Thymus serpyllum 'Albus'
Wild ginger	Asarum
Wild strawberry	Fragaria
Wilton carpet juniper	Juniperus 'Wiltonii'
Wintercreeper	Euonymus
Wintergreen	Gaultheria
Woodbine	Parthenocissus
Wood fern	Dryopteris
Woolly speedwell	Veronica incana
Woolly thyme	Thymus pseudolanuginosus or Thymus lanuginosus
Woolly yarrow	Achillea tomentosa
Wormwood	Artemisia
Y	
Yellow archangel	Lamium galeobdolon
Yellow-root	Xanthorhiza simplicissima

Achillea
Woolly yarrow

Woolly yarrow *(A. tomentosa)* is an evergreen herb with narrow, soft, feathery, gray-green leaves 1 to 4 inches long. Growth habit is spreading and rapid. Tight clumps form a dense, matlike cover 1 to 3 inches high. From spring through summer 2- to 3-inch-wide clusters of tiny yellow blossoms appear in profusion at the top of 4- to 10-inch stems. Periodic cutting helps maintain flower production. Hardy to −45°.

CULTURE. Woolly yarrow is a sturdy, sun-loving, low-maintenance plant that grows successfully in almost any well-drained soil and requires only moderate watering during the summer. Propagate by seed or division. Set out already rooted plants 6 to 12 inches apart, preferably in spring. Cut stems back to the ground in fall at the end of the blooming period.

USES. Woolly yarrow is commonly used in rock gardens and as a border. It can provide erosion control on moderate slopes. Mowed lightly, it becomes an interesting lawn substitute where there is little or no traffic and no desire for flowers.

Adiantum
Five-finger fern

A. pedatum is a hardy maidenhair fern native throughout most of North America. Fronds are delicate in appearance but are wiry, growing to 2 feet high. The plant spreads with creeping root stalks making a beautiful, fine-textured ground cover.

CULTURE. Moist, cool soil with a leaf mold mulch is necessary to keep the delicate, fibrous roots from drying out. Some shade is best although considerable sun is tolerated.

USES. This fern will naturalize well with wild flowers in a native garden. It also thrives in the shade of the taller-growing rhododendrons and similar shrubs, or tucked into the pockets of a stone wall.

Aegopodium
Goutweed, bishop's weed

Goutweed *(A. podagraria)* is a hardy and widely used deciduous perennial (leaves disappear with winter cold, return in spring). It forms a low, dense, fast-growing mat to 6 inches high. Leaves are delicate in appearance, in shades of white and blue-green. Carrotlike flower heads (12-18 inches high) appear in June and produce seed that germinates wherever it lands. Goutweed is very vigorous and apt to become a weed if not controlled. Variegated goutweed *(A. p. 'Variegatum')* is somewhat less vigorous and the most widely planted form.

CULTURE. Goutweed grows in either sun or shade but growth is slower in the shade, making it more manageable. It's quite hardy (to −35°) and tolerates both drought and poor soil. Even a small piece of the creeping roots will start a new plant, the most common method of propagation.

USES. Seldom seen in nurseries, this plant has been passed on by friends and neighbors. Management is easiest when planted between barriers such as a sidewalk and house foundation. Mowing two or three times a season keeps it low, even, and the leaves small and compact.

Aegopodium podagraria

Aegopodium podagraria *'Variegatum'*

Achillea tomentosa

Ajuga
Bugleweed

The ajugas are hardy perennials, long favored by gardeners for their ease of cultivation, fast growth, and showy flowers. There are three species:

The Geneva or alpine bugle, *A. genevensis,* is more a rock garden plant than ground cover. It has no runners and grows in a matlike clump. Flowers are blue, rose, or white.

A. pyramidalis is another clump-forming type having no runners. Leaves are large, clear green with violet flowers. The cultivar 'Metallica Crispa' has metallic reddish-brown leaves with crisped edges.

The ajuga most commonly used as a ground cover is carpet bugle *(A. reptans).* It's fast growing, spreading by creeping stems. It is excellent for a shade ground cover (leaves become larger, more succulent) and will also accept full sun. Foliage consists of tight clusters of somewhat oval, wavy, 2- to 4-inch-long leaves that form a thick, low mat. For a short time in the spring, flower spikes rise 4 to 6 inches above the foliage. The many cultivars of carpet bugle include:

'Atropurpurea': bronze leaves and blue flowers.

'Giant Bronze'; somewhat larger and more vigorous; leaves a metallic bronze.

'Giant Green': same as above but leaves a bright, crisp green.

'Jungle Green': larger, more rounded leaves; flower spikes 8 to 10 inches; a crisp green.

'Jungle Bronze': Slightly smaller leaves are more rounded; growth is more rounded.

'Rubra': dark, purplish leaves.

'Variegata': leaves edged and mottled with pale yellow.

CULTURE. The ajugas grow best in light shade. Good garden soil with fast drainage is necessary, or nematodes and fungus disease are likely to appear. Propagate by division. Plant in spring or fall, spacing 6 to 12 inches apart. Water moderately, more in full sun — plants should not be allowed to dry out. In cold-winter areas, some protection from winter winds is advised. Plants are rejuvenated by mowing lightly after blooming. Ajugas are hardy to —10°.

USES. Carpet bugle is particularly effective when planted in the semi-shade of other plants or building eaves. Use it to fill in beneath foundation shrubs or as a cover for the taller-growing bulbs. Along a path it offers a cool, somewhat formal effect. Flowers are a short-term bonus, its landscape value is based on handsome leaves.

Akebia
Five-leaf akebia

A. quinata is a hardy, gracefully twining shrub. Semi-evergreen and a vigorous grower (3 to 15 feet each year) in mild climates. No insect or disease problems. Delicate leaves on 3- to 5-inch stalks are divided into fives like fingers on a hand. Leaves stay on late into the season, even in the North. Deep green in color 2 to 3 inches long. Rosy-purple flowers in spring, sometimes followed by an edible but insipid fruit. Hardy to —20°.

CULTURE. Thrives in sun or shade and well-drained soil, spaced at 2-foot intervals. Propagated by seeds,

Ajuga reptans

Ajuga reptans

Ajuga reptans

cuttings, and root division. Deep-growing roots hold the soil and withstand drought. Its billowy carpet is successful rambling over slopes or open areas. Should be planted away from low-growing shrubs as its aggressive habit can smother them.

Alyssum
Basket-of-gold, gold-dust, madwort

Basket-of-gold *(A. saxatile* sometimes *Aurinia)* is a hardy perennial (to —30°) and classic rock garden plant best known for its bright, golden yellow flower clusters in early spring. It grows to about 12 inches high and the grayish-green leaves are 2 to 5 inches long.

CULTURE. Basket-of-gold is easily raised from seed but is tap-rooted so should be transplanted while still young. It self-sows freely once established in the garden. Give it full sun and a warm spot in the garden. Most well-drained soils (on the dry side) are acceptable but if soil is very rich, growth is more coarse. Stimulate compact growth by cutting back stems after flowering. Plant 10 to 12 inches apart.

USES. Generally, a prominent spot in the front of the garden or border is best. We grow it in containers and move it to where it suits us best.

Andromeda
Bog rosemary

The virtue of *A. polifolia* is that it grows in wet, acidic soils where little else will. It's evergreen and hardy, (—50°) growing to about 1 foot. Leathery leaves are 1½ inches long. In April or May clusters of tiny china-pink flowers appear at the branch tips. Andromeda spreads by underground runners. Varieties available include 'Nana' and 'Montana' which are lower and more compact.

CULTURE. Andromeda grows easily wherever cranberries grow. (It's natural habitat is a bog.) Full sun is best but some shade is accepted. Propagate by layering or cutting sections of the creeping roots.

USES. Soils that are difficult for most plants are required by this one. In rock gardens where difficult conditions prevail, they do very well.

Arabis
Rock cress

The rock cresses are typically border and rock garden plants, are easily grown, and flower in spring or early summer. Two varieties are good small-space ground covers.

Alpine or mountain rock cress *(A. alpina)* is very hardy — it tolerates temperatures to —35°. In spring,

fragrant white flowers are borne in such profusion that foliage is completely hidden below them. Leaves are evergreen and smooth. Height is 5 to 10 inches.

Wall rock cress *(A. caucasica)* is the more common type. In fact, plants sold as *A. alpina* are often this one. Distinguish them by the fine, feltlike whitish hairs on the leaves of *A. caucasica.* They make the leaves more grayish. Flowers are equally profuse and fragrant. Hardy to —5°.

CULTURE. Rock cress needs full sun and heat. Once established, very little water is required. Plants are essentially drought tolerant. After flowering, cut back the upright stems to induce more horizontal growth. One plant will cover a square foot. Propagate by seeds, cuttings, and division.

USES. These are not large-scale ground covers but are perfect "nook and cranny" plants. For slopes, spilling over walls, or tucked between stones, they are perfectly suited. They combine well with aubrieta, *Phlox subulata,* and *Alyssum (Aurinia) saxatile.* Try them in containers too.

Arctostaphylos
Bearberry, kinnikinnick

Most species of arctostaphylos, commonly known as manzanita, are shrubs or small trees native to the hills and coastal areas of California. But few species are low-growing and make an attractive ground cover. Probably the best for this purpose is *A. uva-ursi,* which grows around the world in northern latitudes. It is a

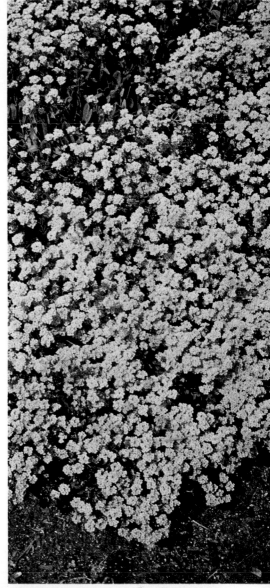

Akebia quinata

Alyssum saxatile

Arabis alpina

Arabis alpina

Arctostaphylos uva-ursi

sturdy, drought-resistant, slow-growing, creeping plant that grows 6 to 10 inches high. In the spring, white or light pink, bell-shaped flowers appear at the end of branches which can spread to 15 feet. Branches are covered with oval, leathery, bright green leaves to 1 inch long that turn red where winters are cold. Two handsome cultivars are 'Point Reyes,' characterized by somewhat darker green leaves set more closely together on shiny red stems, and 'Radiant,' notable for a heavy crop of bright red berries that appear in fall and last most of the winter.

There are other arctostaphylos species useful as ground covers. One is *A. edmundsii,* a northern California native that is more heat- and drought-resistant than *A. uva-ursi.* Among all manzanita ground covers, *A. edmundsii* 'Carmel Sur' is the fastest growing, forming a dense, 8- to 10-inch-high ground cover.

CULTURE. *A. uva-ursi* and its cultivars prefer cooler, more moist conditions than the taller-growing species. In Southern California, they do better in partial shade. To look attractive in the home garden, they need summer watering once every 4 to 6 weeks in loose, fast-draining soil, less in heavy soil. Propagate by seed, cuttings, or division. Set out rooted plants in spring 6 inches or less apart to reduce development of weeds. Except for pruning out dead areas, plants should be left untouched. Hardy to —40° to —50°.

USES. Effective as a large-scale

Arctostaphylos uva-ursi

planting in informal or native gardens, particularly on slopes or trailing over a wall. Tea made from kinnikinick contains arbutin, useful as a disinfectant.

Arenaria
Moss sandwort

A. verna (caespitosa) is a mossy perennial sometimes erroneously called Irish moss (see *Sagina subulata*). It has small, narrow, dark green leaves that form a dense, slowly spreading, 3-inch mat. Tiny white flowers appear in the summer. Several varieties offer light variations in the color of the foliage.

CULTURE. Moss sandwort grows in most well-drained soils, preferably in part shade. It needs regular watering, with the amount increased the more it is exposed to full sun. It is best propagated by dividing plants in the

spring. The plant is hardy (—50°) but needs some winter protection in cold, exposed locations.

USES. Between stepping stones, in rock gardens, or as accent clumps bordering wall. See page 94 for a photo of a Scotch and Irish moss "checker board." Light traffic.

Armeria
Thrift, sea pink

The appearance of *A. maritima* varies, depending on soil conditions, exposure, and variety. Because of the number of varieties and natural hybridization, you cannot always be certain from names given to young plants just precisely what you may end up with. Common varieties are *'alba'* (white flowers), *'californica'* (shorter stems, larger flowers), and *'purpurea'* (purple flowers). There are many others.

Common thrift is a sturdy, evergreen perennial that characteristically grows in dense, grassy clumps from which an abundance of tightly clustered, delicate pink or white flowers, ¾ inch across, appear at the end of long, thin stems. Height can range from 2-inch tufts and 3- to 5-inch stems, to 10-inch tufts with flowers rising above 2 feet. Growth rate is slow. Thrift blooms continuously in the spring, into summer in inland areas, even longer in coastal and cooler areas. Clumps spread to about 15 inches.

CULTURE. Thrift will grow in almost any soil, but needs good drainage and full sun to thrive. Maintenance is low, requiring only moderate watering during hot summer months. To insure accurate reproduction, plants are best propagated by division. Very hardy, tolerates temperatures to −50°.

USES. Typically used in rock gardens, as borders, and edgings. A desirable plant by reason of its general toughness, long bloom, delicacy of flowers, and interesting leaf texture. Kept low, it becomes ideal for use between stepping stones.

Artemisia
Dusty-miller, wormwood, angel's hair

Artemisias are sturdier-than-they-look perennial herbs characterized by lacy, silver-gray, finely cut foliage, and tiny, inconspicuous yellow flower heads that appear for a short time at summer's end.

Caucasian wormwood (A. caucasica) sold at some nurseries under the name 'Silver Spreader' forms a dense mat 3 to 6 inches high that spreads 2 feet or more. The foliage of fringed wormwood is more white and is carried on the upper part of 12- to 18-inch stems that are woody below. A. schmidtiana forms dense, tufted mounds; two varieties differing only in height are 'Silver Mound,' about a foot tall, and 'Nana' a few inches tall. Hardy to −25°.

CULTURE. These plants will thrive in almost any well-drained soil in full sun or part shade, but preferably in sun. They are drought-tolerant, only needing moderate watering. Tall varieties should be cut back as they become rangy. Propagation by seed is slow; better by division. Plant in spring, placing low varieties 6 inches apart, taller varieties 12 inches apart.

USES. These are accent plants, typically effective as borders in places where their soft, pale color and interesting leaf pattern contrast with bright-colored plants. A "something different" plant.

Asarum
Wild ginger

The wild gingers are incomparable ground covers for the heavily shaded, woodland soils to which they are native. Although not related to culinary ginger, the creeping rootstalks and pungent leaves have a gingerlike fragrance. They have 2- to 7-inch heart-shaped leaves on 7- to 10-inch stalks. Flowers are minute and appear in early spring. There are several species, both deciduous and evergreen, with variations in leaf size and coloring.

Armeria maritima

Armeria maritima

Artemisia schmidtiana

Artemisia 'Silver Dust'

Astilbe <del>+W·RM AOT</del> Asarum europeum

Astilbe

Asarum shuttleworthii

USES. In a naturalistic woodland garden, ginger forms an exceptionally attractive, dense mat. Combine them with evergreen shrubs or wild flowers.

Asparagus
Sprenger asparagus fern

Sprenger asparagus (A. densiflorus 'Sprengeri') is one of several species of ornamental asparagus admired for their fernlike foliage. Commonly a container plant, its trailing growth habit and arching sprays of light green, needle-like leaves make it useful as a ground cover in certain situations. Clusters of tiny, pinkish-white flowers appear in spring and into summer, followed by equally small, bright red berries that soon begin to fall. The growth rate is moderate and the plant can be expected to billow up to about 18 inches.

CULTURE. Sprenger asparagus grows well in full sun or light shade and in moist soils. This is a sturdy, drought-

A. caudatum (British Columbia wild ginger) is evergreen and probably most commonly available. It's native to the coastal mountains of the western United States and British Columbia. A. europeaum (European wild ginger) is virtually identical to A. caudatum except for its more shiny, glossy leaves. Both are hardy to −25°. Other evergreens are A. arifolium and A. virginicum. They are similar except for reduced cold tolerance (to −5 or −10°). They are native to the southeastern U.S.

Deciduous types are native over much of the eastern United States. A. canadense (Canadian wild ginger) was used as a ginger substitute by collecting and drying the creeping roots. It's one of the most hardy, tolerating temperatures to −35°.

A. shuttleworthii is similar but has thinner, mottled, usually larger leaves and is hardy to zero. Deciduous forms are not cultivated as frequently as the evergreen ones because of the lack of winter effect.

CULTURE. The gingers are native to woodlands where shade is heavy and the soil is high in humus and moisture. With lots of water they will grow in heavy soils, but do best in either native or generously amended soil. Locations protected from drying winds are best. Propagate by division of the creeping rootstalks.

Asparagus densiflorus 'Sprengeri'

Asparagus densiflorus 'Sprengeri'

Athyrium

Athyriums are deciduous, delicate, 2- to 4-foot ferns. They are unusually easy to grow. The most common variety is the lady fern *(A. filix-femina)*. It tolerates more sun and less moisture than most ferns and spreads thickly enough to out-compete most weeds. Its shape is like a vase and fronds are yellow green. For collectors, there are many named varieties.

The Japanese painted fern is *A. goeringianum.* It's lower (to 1½ feet) and has slightly drooping fronds, remarkable for their coloring. Stems and main veins are ruby-red and fronds are a soft gray-green creating a striking contrast. The cultivar 'Pictum' is similar but the central stripe is gray.

CULTURE. The aforementioned are hardy plants that will grow just about anywhere. Protection from wind is advised, or the fronds will become ragged looking. Like most ferns, ideal conditions include a well-prepared soil kept moist, with some shade.

USES. The unusual coloring of the Japanese painted fern makes it an interesting accent plant — use it where it can be appreciated at close range. The lady fern makes an excellent ground cover in woodland gardens or along streams.

Aubrieta
Common aubrieta, stonecress

Aubrieta *(A. deltoides)* is a common rock garden plant used in the same way as arabis, *Phlox subulata, Alyssum saxatile,* and *Iberis semper-virens.* Plants grow between 2 and 6 inches high (can reach 1 foot) and spread to 1 to 1½ feet. Leaves are a warm gray color and ¾-inch flowers range from light rose to deep purple. Hardy to −20°.

CULTURE. Easily grown in full sun (except in hot-summer areas) and typical well-drained soil. It can be killed by being too wet in the winter or too dry in summer. Shear back half way after flowers die and before seeds set. Periodic application of an all-purpose fertilizer is beneficial. Aubrietas are easily grown from seed — sow in late spring for flowers the following spring. Divide (after bloom in spring) or take cuttings in fall, to multiply named selections.

USES. These are commonly used in rock gardens and for edging. Planted in or on top of a loose stone wall, aubrieta will produce a striking, cascade effect. They do particularly well in the North-west and are a commonly used plant in that region.

resistant plant that requires little care but will look better with regular watering and occasional feeding. Propagation is easy by seed or division. As a ground cover, it is restricted to warm-winter areas. Hardy to 25°.

USES. A small area plant. Good in a raised bed where it might cascade over a low wall. Sprenger asparagus has small prickles and a natural tendency to cling to, or climb, other plants. For this reason, it is best grown alone.

Astilbe
False spirea, Meadowsweet

The astilbes are not usually considered ground covers. Still, they are long-lived perennials and we think you'll agree they make a dramatic accent as a small-scale ground cover. The delicate flowers (May to June) are the main attraction. Here are a few of the many varieties and colors available: 'Bridal Veil,' pure white; 'Cattleya,' pink; 'Diamond,' white;

'Deutschland,' creamy white; 'Fanal,' deep garnet-red; 'Peach Blossom,' a pale peach-pink; and 'Rheinland,' carmine-pink.

CULTURE. Astilbes thrive where soil is cool, moist, and rich in humus. They need some shading from intense light. For best flower display, they should be divided every 3 or 4 years and fertilized each spring, but they can stay longer without being divided. Cut back after flowering. Roots are shallow, so deep-working the soil is not necessary, but a mulch is. Soil should be well drained because astilbes are very sensitive to water-logged conditions in winter. (Plant in mounds or raised beds to improve drainage.) In some areas Japanese beetles are a pest of astilbes. Control them with Sevin insecticide.

USES. Astilbes are well adapted near pools and streams. They combine well with hostas and bergenias, and adapt to container culture. Flowers can be forced when grown in a greenhouse.

Berberis
Japanese barberry

Japanese barberry *(B. thunbergii)* is a deciduous, 4- to 8-foot-high shrub, with bright red berries, spiny arching branches, and brilliant yellow to scarlet autumn foliage. A number of cultivated varieties having a low or compact growth habit are suitable for use as ground covers. The most popular, and probably the best, is 'Crimson Pygmy' (often sold as 'Atropurpurea Nana'). It forms a compact mound about a foot high and 2 feet across.

The foliage is composed of blood-red leaves, ½ to 1 inch long, set densely along the branches. The leaves retain their color through spring and summer.

CULTURE. As with most deciduous barberries, *B. thunbergii* and its various cultivars grow well in almost any soil and are very drought tolerant. They require only ordinary garden care. The capacity to withstand neglect and extremes of climate and soil is, perhaps, their most outstanding quality. All perform well in sun or partial shade but red-leaved forms such as 'Crimson Pygmy' need full sun for the best color to develop. Propagation is by seed, layering, or softwood cuttings. Hardy to −20°.

USES. The low-growing or compact cultivars of *B. thunbergii* are excellent for ground cover on gentle slopes, along paths, and in dry, rocky areas. The spiny branches greatly discourage traffic.

Bergenia
Bergenia

These are common but too little appreciated hardy perennials that make dramatic accents in partially shaded areas. Leaves are large, and leathery. Very handsome pink, white, or rose flower spikes appear in spring. Two species are well known.

B. corditolia, heartleaf bergenia, grows to 20 inches high. Leaves are fleshy, to 10 inches long, have wavy, saw-tooth edges, and are heart-shaped where they connect to the stem. Flowers in spring are on spikes about 15 inches tall.

B. crassifolia, Siberian tea, is very similar to *cordifolia* but leaves are shorter by 2 or 3 inches, very finely toothed, and do not have a heart-shaped base. Flower spikes are taller by 3 or 4 inches and bloom in winter in mild-climate areas. Both species, though tender and tropical looking, are fully hardy to −45°.

CULTURE. Bergenias are easily grown and tolerant of neglect but follow these guidelines to best appreciate

Campanula poscharskyana

them. Plant in some shade, protected from wind that can tear the large leaves (in cool, coastal areas full sun is okay). Amend soil for ideal moist and well-drained conditions. Cut back when the thick woody rhizome becomes leggy; if clumps become crowded, divide them. Water and fertilize regularly and bait for slugs and snails.

USES. Commonly used for shady borders, in clumps among smaller-leaved ground covers, or around irregular surfaces, such as rocks, and by pools and streams. They combine well with ferns, hostas, and tall rhododendrons.

Campanula
Bellflower

The two or three hundred species in this genus are characterized by mostly bell-shaped flowers in various shades of blue. 'Adriatic bellflower' *(C. elatines 'garganica'),* usually sold as *C. garganica,* is the lowest-growing. It forms a loose, 3- to 6-inch-high mat made up of heart-shaped serrated green leaves, 1½ inches wide, growing at the ends of spreading stems. Violet-blue flowers, flat and star-shaped rather than bell-shaped, appear singly, but in profusion, from late summer into fall. Serbian bellflower *(C. poscharskyana)* is similar but taller, reaching up to a foot, and its flowers, also star-shaped, have a more lavender hue. It has a trailing growth habit, spreading rapidly by creeping runners.

CULTURE. These bellflowers are sturdy plants that grow well in almost any soil having good drainage. In cold climates and coastal areas they grow best in full sun; in warmer climates they need light shade. In dry-summer areas they require watering two or three times a month. Propagate them by seed or by dividing plants in the spring, spacing plants about 10 inches apart. Very hardy; tolerates cold to −40°. These plants can be invasive and should be contained or separated from other plants by a redwood header or divider.

USES. The following bellflowers are for small-scale planting; both need to be seen up close to be appreciated. *C. elatines 'garganica'* is very attractive under the filtered shade of a large tree, such as a sycamore, where it can also nudge up against exposed roots. It is also effective spilling over a stone wall. *C. poscharskyana* is lovely as an accent plant in any shaded garden area.

Cerastium
Snow-in-summer

C. tomentosum is a deservedly popular ground cover by virtue of its striking light gray foliage, its toughness, and its adaptability to almost any growing condition. A dense mat 4 to 6 inches high is formed by masses of slender stems that spread along the ground and then turn upward, their upper parts covered by narrow, ¾-inch-long woolly leaves. From spring into summer the foliage is covered by masses of ½ inch white flowers. Growth rate is fairly rapid, a single plant spreading about 2 feet in a year.

CULTURE. For optimum appearance, snow-in-summer needs full sun and soil with good drainage. It is drought resistant but, again, will look better with once-a-week watering in hot, dry-summer areas. Propagation is easy by seed, division or cuttings. Plant 1 to 2 feet apart in spring. A planting can be lightly mowed at the end of the flowering period to remove dead flower heads. It is very hardy, able to withstand temperatures to −40°.

USES. Good for large or small-scale planting wherever its unusual color will stand in contrast to its surroundings. Equally good on slopes or level ground, or used between stepping stones.

Ceratostigma
Blue leadwort, dwarf plumbago

C. plumbaginoides is an easy-to-grow, wiry-stemmed perennial. It's valued for its long-lasting, ½-inch blue flowers that come in midsummer, lasting until fall. Height rarely exceeds 12 inches. It spreads vigorously by underground stems. Leaves are dark green, about 3 inches long, and have a reddish tint in the fall. In the mildest climates, some leaves will remain throughout winter but most usually die to the ground and reappear by late spring. Hardy to −10°.

CULTURE. Many soil types are tolerated as long as drainage is good. Takes full sun if water is plentiful, otherwise shade is better. The only

Berberis thunbergii

Berberis thunbergii, *with bright green* Arctostaphylos uva-ursi.

Bergenia cordifolia

Campanula poscharskyana

Campanula

Chamaemelum nobile

CULTURE. Grows best in light, sandy soil in full sun; tolerates some shade. Deep roots make it drought-resistant, requiring only moderate watering in summer. Easily propagated by division. Start new planting in spring or fall from divisions set 6 to 12 inches apart. Hardy to 0°.

USES. Left to grow to its natural height, chamomile is an adaptive plant in small areas in the garden. Sheared, it is attractive between stepping stones. Mowed and rolled, it can be a lawn substitute or a living, growing path, made more attractive by the pleasant fragrance it gives off when walked on. If you like herb teas, the dried flower heads of chamomile make one of the finest. Steep them in hot water (not boiling) for 10 to 15 minutes. It only lightly colors the water — judge strength by smelling. Traditionally, it's a relaxing bedtime drink. Legend has it that chamomile is the only known cure for nightmares.

maintenance is cutting back after flowering in the spring before new growth starts. Spaced 1 to 2 feet apart, they will quickly fill in.

USES. These are adaptable plants with many potential uses. They can cover fairly large areas but are also attractive tucked in corners or under shrubs. Combines well with English boxwood, ajuga, or sempervivums.

Chamaemelum
Chamomile

Chamomile (C. nobile, formerly known as Anthemis nobilis) is the evergreen perennial herb long popular in Europe as a lawn substitute. It's also famous for the herbal tea made from dried flower heads. During summer, small greenish or yellowish flower heads with white petals appear at the top of slender stalks. Chamomile is distinguished by lacy, finely cut, lustrous grass-green leaves that form a soft mat 1 to 8 inches high. It spreads at a moderate rate, rooting as stolons or runners advance.

Chrysanthemum
Feverfew

Feverfew (C. parthenium) will grow in a crack in the driveway and persist even after it has presumably been ripped out. It is a leafy, upright ornamental with great numbers of small (¼- to ½-inch) white daisy flowers that bloom throughout the summer. C. parthenium grows 2 to 3 feet high. Varieties include 'Golden Ball,' yellow flowers; 'Silver Ball,' double flower forms in white; and 'Golden Feather,' chartreuse foliage, 8 to 10 inches high.

CULTURE. C. parthenium self-sows freely or, like the varieties, can be propagated by division. The varieties can also be propagated by seeds. These plants can be sheared occasionally to keep them low and more compact. Hardy to −10°F.

USES. Chiefly used as a filler or for contrast among other bedding plants. Tea made from the flower heads was at one time taken medicinally to reduce fever, hence its popular name.

Comptonia
Sweet fern

Not a true fern, sweet fern (C. peregrina) is a deciduous shrub native to eastern North America woodlands. The toothed, narrow, fernlike leaves are fragrant. Normal height is 1½ to 2 feet but some may reach 5 feet. It combines well with the low-growing junipers. Sweet fern spreads by underground roots that become very tightly knit, which has made it popular for erosion control by highway departments. Hardy to −50°.

Cornus stolonifera

CULTURE. Sweet ferns grow in either wet or dry soil (acidic is best) but must have full sun. Can be difficult to transplant — large clumps are best. Plant in early spring, cutting back stems to the base and spacing about 2 feet apart.

USES. This plant is a good choice for erosion control on banks. The leaves also make a pleasant tea.

Conifers

Aside from the junipers, there are few prostrate conifers suitable as ground covers. Usually conifers are not massed as junipers but used as specimen or accent plants. They are evergreen and grow very slowly, so little maintenance is necessary. For formal gardens, around rocks, draping over low walls, and softening hard edges, they do very well. Following are brief descriptions of some of the best.

The deodar cedar is familiar as an 80-foot tree. The selection 'Repandens' *(Cedrus deodara* 'Repandens') is strongly pendulous and usually grows no taller than 2½ feet.

The Norway spruce, *Picea abies,* is a tree that can grow to over 100 feet. They're hardy almost everywhere — to −50°. The selection 'Clanbrasiliana' is a widely adaptable (and available) form that grows to just 2 feet wide in 20 years. Branchlets are thin and shiny white.

P. a. 'Procumbens' grows no higher than 3½ feet. Its branchlets are thin, stiff, and light yellow.

P. a. 'Repens' is commonly known as the creeping Norway spruce. It becomes much more broad than its 1½-foot height. Branchlets are thin and yellowish-green. A fine rock garden plant.

The pine, *Pinus strobus* 'Prostrata' is very hardy (−35°) but may need protection from wind. The main stem "knuckles" slightly above the soil, spreading out horizontal branches. It will hang vertically over the face of a stone wall.

The Mugho pine, *Pinus mugo mughus,* is a slow-growing shrub that can be massed or used as a specimen plant. There are several new varieties to choose from. When making your selection, look for dense plants that have a pleasing form. Pruning the candles will keep it dense; removing

Dianthus

entire candle in spring will force side growth to continue. Removing less of the candle will check growth but not as severely.

The yews are less hardy than the spruces or pines but are very popular and much used as ground cover plants. The English yew, *Taxus baccata,* is familiar sheared as hedges and as estate specimens. It grows slowly so doesn't require frequent pruning to be neat. The selection 'Repandens' grows no taller than 2 feet. The dark, flat, shining leaves are somewhat sickle-shaped and dull green beneath. This is among the hardiest forms, accepting temperatures to −10°.

Convallaria
Lily-of-the-valley

Lily-of-the-valley *(C. majalis)* is one of the most hardy and adaptable ground covers. It thrives in partial or full shade and develops a dense mass of soil-holding roots. Leaves die back in the fall and are renewed in spring. New leaves grow to 8 inches long and 1 to 3 inches wide. The fragrant, ¼-inch, usually white, bell-shaped flowers come in spring. These are fully hardy plants (to −40°) but do not thrive in mild-climate areas. There are selections available such as 'Fortins Giant,' larger flowers, and 'Rosea,' pale pink flowers.

CULTURE: These are undemanding plants that grow in just about any soil. Planted on 7-inch centers, plants spread and make a ground cover that needs almost no attention. Periodic feeding will improve them. Divide the clumps anytime. Divisions, called pips, can be planted out to increase your own supply or to share with neighbors.

USES: Lillies-of-the-valley are deciduous, best where the lack of winter won't be missed. Typically, they are used around shrubs like the taller rhododendrons or camellias. They are also effective with ferns.

Cornus
Bunchberry, red-osier dogwood

There are two relatives of the well-known dogwood tree that are useful as ground covers: bunchberry *(C. canadensis)* and red-osier dogwood *(C. sericea).*

The bunchberry is native from Alaska to New Mexico to West Virginia, always growing in cool, moist, acidic soil. In open woodlands, it can be found covering an area up to a square mile. It spreads (not invasively) by underground runners and rarely grows taller than 9 inches. Tiny flower clusters appear in early spring and are surrounded by four or six white bracts. Bright red fruits mature by late summer and last until eaten by birds. Oval leaves are 3 inches in length, a deep rich green in summer, then turn yellow to red in the fall.

The red-osier dogwood is a deciduous, spreading shrub that grows to 5 to 7 feet in height. It is appreciated for its winter color of bright red twigs. Its best use is on banks or in wet soils. Pruning the branches to the ground every three or four years will produce more brightly colored twigs. The selection 'Kelseyi' is a dwarf form that rarely exceeds 2 feet and 'Flaviramea' has yellow twigs.

CULTURE. Bunchberries have an undeserved reputation for being difficult to establish. For the best chance of success, don't skimp on soil preparation. The soil should be loose and acidic with much leafmold, pine needles, or peat worked in; transplant whole sods (if possible) in 5- or 6-square-foot sections. Plant in a site that is cool and moist but with plenty of springtime sun (such as under deciduous trees).

USES. Once established, these are plants of rare beauty. Bunchberry does well in woodland and mountain gardens, and as a ground cover around rhododendrons and similar plants.

The red-osier dogwood is coarse and taller growing but does spread and becomes quite dense. Because of the periodic pruning that needs to be done, use it in small, manageable clumps.

Coronilla
Crown vetch

The deep, soil-building roots and dense, weed-choking, 2-foot top growth of crown vetch *(C. varia)* have made this one of the most popular ground covers for erosion control. The highway departments between Illinois and Pennsylvania have used it extensively. It dies back in winter and the mass of brown stems can be a fire hazard in some areas. Leaves consist of many ½-inch oval leaflets. Pinkish flowers appear in summer. Crown vetch is very hardy (to −40°).

CULTURE: Crown vetch can be planted by seed, using about 1 pound per 1,000 square feet. Transplanting crowns (on 2' centers) or whole sods are other, more reliable, ways to establish a cover. Once established, fertilizer is not needed particularly. Crown vetch is drought-resistant, prefers full sun, but tolerates some

Draping Picea

Pinus mugo mughus

Picea abies 'Procumbens'

Picea pungens 'Glauca prostrata'

shade. It spreads by underground runners, so it can be invasive and difficult to eradicate. If possible, mow in spring (a sharp rotary or flail-type mower) and it will make a beautiful green summer carpet.

USES. Over large, no-maintenance areas, crown vetch does an excellent job. Erosion control is a prime use. Honeybees use the flowers and cattle eat the foliage.

Cotoneaster
Cotoneaster

There are many cotoneasters suitable as ground covers. Among them are varieties adapted to virtually every climate of North America. They are deep-rooted and good soil binders, each variety producing attractive flowers in spring and berries in fall.

Creeping cotoneaster (C. adpressus) is a deciduous type that will eventually reach 1 foot high, spreading 6 feet. Small, ¼-inch flowers are pink-tinted; red fruits are the same size. Leaves are small (½ inch) and dark green. Early cotoneaster (C.a. 'praecox') is more vigorous and slightly larger. It becomes taller — to 1½ feet, with slightly larger leaves and berries.

Creeping cotoneaster is noted for its short, rigid branches and dense, low habit. Hardy to —20°.

Cranberry cotoneaster (C. apiculatus) is very similar to the more common rock cotoneaster. It differs mainly by its larger berries that remain on the plant throughout winter. A deciduous plant, it grows to 1 to 2 feet high and spreads to 4 or 5 feet. Flowers are pinkish and in clusters; leaves are nearly round, usually less than ½ inch in diameter, and slightly hairy on the bottom side. Hardy to —20°.

The Himalyan or Pyrenees cotoneaster (C. congestus) is evergreen. It is slow growing to about 3 feet and will spread 3 feet in 5 years. Flowers are small, whitish-pink and appear in June. Berries are bright red; leaves are similar to the rockspray cotoneaster but more rounded and without the fine hairs. The Himalayan cotoneaster is one of the hardy evergreens. Because of their slow growth rate, they are very easy to take care of once they are established. Hardy to —5°.

The necklace cotoneaster (C. conspicuus 'decorus') is an extremely prostrate evergreen form. Secondary branches grow vertically up to 1 to 1½ feet. Ultimate spread is 6 to 8 feet. Flowers are white and berries are fairly large, covering the branches in the fall. Leaves are small

(¼ inch), dark green on top with paler undersides.

Necklace cotoneaster is a good ground cover but is not dense enough to shade out weeds. Best used in containers or rock gardens. Hardy to 0°.

Bearberry cotoneaster (C. dammeri) is distinct on two counts: it's the flattest of the cotoneasters, spreading 10 feet and only becoming ½ to 1 foot tall. Also, it's the hardiest of the evergreen type of cotoneaster ground covers. It tolerates temperatures to —10°. Flowers are white and the masses of bright red fruits are highly ornamental. Leaves are 1 inch long and oval shaped, glossy green above and pale, sometimes whitish beneath. There are two varieties of this plant: 'Lowfast,' a very fast-growing ground cover, possessing slightly smaller leaves more widely spaced on the branches.

'Skogsholmen' (or bearberry cotoneaster), a Swedish selection, is similarly vigorous and fast growing but is also noted for its springtime flower display. These are handsome but uneven woody plants, neat all year and fine for close-up viewing. One of the very best for following surface contours, or cascading over walls.

The rock cotoneaster (C. horizontalis) is perhaps the most widely grown of all. It's semievergreen in mild climates, losing leaves for only a short time; elsewhere it's deciduous but so heavily covered with bright red berries that leaves aren't missed. Mass plantings maintain a 3- to 4-foot height. Branches eventually spread to 8 or 10 feet, sometimes more. Flowers and fruit are small, leaves are round, ½ inch in diameter, and become reddish in color before falling.

Rock cotoneaster is good in combination with low-growing junipers. It's

Convallaria majalis

Violets in foreground combine with Dicentra.

heavily textured and especially effective on banks and in low dividers to discourage traffic. Hardy to —20°.

The smallest-leaved, finest-textured type is the rockspray or small-leaved cotoneaster *(C. microphyllus),* an evergreen that spreads trailing branches to 6 feet; smaller branches grow upright to 2 or 3 feet. White flowers appear in June; scarlet-red berries mature in the fall. Leaves are small, ¼-½ inch long, shiny green on top. Fine hairs give the underside of the leaf a grayish cast.

There are three forms of this species: 'Cochleatus' is a more dwarf form. You can recognize it by the broad-at-the-tip, spoon-shaped leaves. The leaf edges are sometimes rolled upwards. It is an interesting plant often used for bonsai. *'Thymifolius'* is a very compact form and has stiff, upright branches. It's small enough for the rock garden. 'Emerald Spray' is resistant to fire blight, a disease that sometimes attacks cotoneasters.

The tangled, intermingling stems of rockspray are well suited for banks or around rocks. This variety must be thriving to look acceptable, benefiting from soil amendments before planting. This plant is a popular variety in the South. Hardy to —10°.

CULTURE. Cotoneasters are tough and hardy plants. They're easy to grow, transplant, and care for, thriving in heavy clay soil.

Some pests can be damaging to cotoneasters. Watch out for scale, red spiders and lace bugs. (See page 91.) Fire blight, a bacterial disease, also attacks cotoneasters. Leaves suddenly wilt on an infected twig, turn brown, but don't fall off. Spray flowers every 4 to 5 days with bordeaux fixed copper, or streptomycin spray. When pruning these dead branches, cut at least 4 inches into apparently healthy wood; the disease is present beyond the damaged area. To avoid spreading the disease, burn diseased wood and disinfect pruning tools after use with a five percent bleach solution.

Very little pruning of cotoneasters is necessary, but occasionally dead or

Cotoneaster

The cotoneasters are easy-to-grow plants, able to thrive in many different situations. These photographs demonstrate some of their landscaping possibilities.

At right, a casual effect is created by cotoneaster draping over a stairway. Below, cranberry cotoneaster C. apiculatus *displays its winter show of bright red berries.*

awkward branches need to be removed. Otherwise prune only to encourage the graceful arching of the branches. Don't use hedge shears — the stubbed branches are unattractive.

Cotula
New Zealand brass buttons

C. squalida is an evergreen, herbaceous perennial with delicate, fernlike foliage and small, dull greenish-yellow flower heads ("brass buttons") that are produced heavily during the summer. Individual leaves are finely divided, bronze-green in color, and covered with soft hairs. The plant grows 2 to 3 inches high and creeps fairly rapidly along the ground for a foot or more. The creep-

ing stems root along their length to form a thick dense carpet, thus their value as a lawn substitute.

CULTURE. *Cotula squalida* grows best in moist, rich soil and in full sun to light shade. In areas where temperatures drop to zero degrees, the foliage dies back for a time but will recover quickly when warm weather returns. Propagate by division in spring. Set out new plants 4 to 6 inches apart.

USES. This species is tough and can withstand considerable traffic. It makes an unusual, rather attractive alternative to grass or dichondra for small-scale lawns. It also can be used effectively as a ground cover between stones on paths and in rock gardens.

Cytisus
Broom

Ground cover brooms include the members of two genera (see Genista). The Scotch brooms, cytisus are the best known to most gardeners. Some varieties have naturalized on both the Atlantic and Pacific Coasts and are particularly visible in early spring covered with yellow, sweet pealike flowers.

One of the most useful ground brooms is the Kew broom, *C. kewensis*. It grows only 6 to 10 inches high but spreads 3 feet in each direction. The trailing branches are handsome cascading over low walls. Leaves are tiny and usually divided into three

Bearberry cotoneaster, (C. dammeri) above, is the lowest growing species, and also the hardiest, to −10°. At right, a low formal hedge grows parallel to a group of slash pines. Below, as a "transition" plant, blending lawn with trees. C. horizontalis, far right, is the most widely used, growing to 2 to 3 feet in height.

leaflets. Pale yellow ½-inch flowers appear in May.

Prostrate broom, *C. decumbens,* is another very good ground cover. It differs only slightly from the Kew broom. Flowers are colored bright yellow and they come later in the season by a few weeks. It is also more hardy; *C. kewensis* is hardy to —5° and *C. decumbens* to —10°.

CULTURE. Brooms are very adaptable plants. Generally they do best in dry, poor, slightly acidic soil. If drainage is good, plentiful water is accepted such as in the Northwest, where brooms thrive. The greatest difficulty growing them is getting them started or transplanted. Start with young, cutting-grown plants in flats or containers. Once they are established, they require little or no care. Hard or softwood cuttings taken in

August root best. Little pruning is necessary but if plants become spindly, cut back after flowering.

USES. These are excellent plants for hot, dry, sunny locations. In the Southwest, they combine well with many of the drought-tolerant natives. A good coastal plant, they tolerate salt-laden air and do well in sandy soil. The plants are very effective trailing over walls and down slopes.

Dianthus
Pinks

There are at least a hundred species and many more hybrids of pinks, almost all having in common a spicy, usually clovelike scent, single or double flowers 1½ to 3 inches across and white or pink to deep red in color. Grass, cottage, or Scotch pink *(D. plumarius),* is a relatively low-growing perennial that blooms

from late May through summer. It has small single or double flowers on stems rising 15 inches above a grass-like turf made of 3-inch needle-tipped leaves. Hardy to —10°.

Maiden pink *(D. deltoides)* makes an excellent carpet of blue-green grasslike leaves. One of the most common, it grows to 6 inches, but can be kept to 2 to 3 inches by mowing. Blooms in June. It's very hardy, to —50°.

Sandy pink *(D. arenarius)* grows taller than maiden pink and is slightly less hardy, but will tolerate some shade. Height, unmowed, reaches 8 or 9 inches; reliably hardy to —35° or —40°.

CULTURE. Pink fanciers say the best way to grow them is from seed, but they can also be grown from cuttings or by division. Space 10″ to 12″ apart. They need full sun, a light soil (preferably with some lime) and good drainage. Mow after flowering to maintain even, compact growth.

USES. Pinks are classic edging and rock garden plants and have been favored as bouquets for at least 300 years.

Dicentra
Fringed bleeding-heart

Fringed bleeding-heart *(D. eximia),* native to the Northeast, is an easily grown perennial perfectly suited to beautifying shady corners. Not a ground cover for large areas, they form 2-foot clumps 1 to 2 feet high (often higher in shade). The heart-shaped pink flowers are attached to 12-inch spikes that appear in May and last until August. Leaves are fernlike and a blue or gray-green color. Of the many selections available, 'Bountiful' is one of the best with darker green foliage and rich pink flowers. Fringed bleeding-heart is hardy to —40°.

CULTURE. Most well-drained soils are acceptable but a rich humus is best. Some shade is advisable unless the soil is unusually moist. To make a solid cover, plant clumps about 8 inches apart. Propagate by seed or by division in early spring. Seedlings sometimes sprout nearby — these readily self-sow. Cut back in July or August to stimulate dense foliage growth and possibly another flowering in the fall.

USES. This is the prefect plant for turning that empty, unused corner into a place of beauty. Bleeding-hearts combine well with ferns and wild flowers. Both the cut foliage and flowers are useful indoors for long-lasting arrangements.

Epimedium

Dicentra exima

Dianthus

Fragaria chiloensis

Dryopteris
Wood fern, shield fern

This is a large group of ferns including many natives of the U.S. and Canadian forests. Most are very hardy, evergreen, and easy to grow.

The florist's fern is *D. austriaca 'spinulosa.'* It is widely distributed throughout eastern North America. Its fronds are harvested in summer and shipped in winter.

A good landscape accent plant also native to the Northeast is the leather wood fern, *D. marginalis.* It grows in clumps to about 2 feet and is hardy to —35°.

The coastal wood fern, *D. arguta* is native to western North America. It grows to about 3 feet.

CULTURE. All wood ferns need shade, moist soil, and a humus-rich soil. Many forms spread by underground runners so are easily propagated by division.

USES. These are special-purpose ground covers, not used to cover large areas but to accent or complete a landscape. They are best in a natural or native garden.

Duchesnea
Indian strawberry, mock strawberry

Indian strawberry *(D. indica)* has a superficial resemblance to *Fragaria chiloensis* but differs in several significant, identifying respects. Its leaves are thinner and smaller and its flowers are yellow. It forms an equally dense, but somewhat lower mat and spreads rapidly by runners like the wild strawberry.

CULTURE. The cultural requirements are the same as for *F. chiloensis* with

Euonymus

Euonymus fortunei 'Minima'

one important difference: it does best in light shade. It is also much hardier, to −30°.

USES. Most attractive as a mass planting among a small grouping of trees or, in smaller areas, in the filtered shade of shrubs.

Epimedium
Barrenwort, bishop's-hat

The epimediums are easy to grow, hardy, and too little used. They spread with creeping roots to make a uniform, nine-inch soil cover. The plant is semievergreen; most of the leathery, heart-shaped leaves die back in winter but a few last into January. In early spring, the new leaves are a pale green with some rose color. During midseason they are a deep, glossy green and in fall they are reddish. Tiny, ½-inch orchidlike flowers (shaped like a bishop's hat) appear in May. Many colors are available and they last well when cut. Epimediums are very hardy, charming, unobstrusive plants. They tolerate temperatures to −35° and −40°.

E. grandiflorum is the most commonly cultivated form. It grows to about 1 foot. Different selections offer different flower colors. 'Rose Queen' has bright, rose-colored flowers with spurs tipped white. The hybrid E. versicolor 'Sulphureum' has yellow flowers. E. youngianum 'Niveum' grows compactly and has white flowers.

Euonymus

CULTURE. These are long-lived, easy-to-grow perennials. Light shade is usually best but full sun is okay if the soil is rich, acidic and moist. The creeping roots are close to the surface so don't cultivate around them. Planted 10 inches apart, they will fill in without overcrowding. To propagate, divide the clumps in early spring. Cut off old leaves so that small flowers and new leaves will be visible.

USES. Epimediums thrive in the light shade of other acid-soil plants such as the taller rhododendrons, camellias, and ferns. Their roots compete very well with tree roots so plant them around trees such as crabapple and magnolia.

Erodium
Heron's-bill, Alpine geranium

E. chamaedryoides is notable for its dense, delicately textured green foliage that grows in clumps 3 to 6 inches high, spreads to about a foot in one season, and turns reddish in winter. Leaves are small, lightly lobed, and ovate. White, pink-veined, ½-inch-wide flowers bloom from spring through summer. A variety with pink flowers veined with red is *E. c.* 'Roseum.' Growth rate is moderate. The plant gets its popular name, heron's-bill, from the ½-inch-long needle-like stalks seen at the ends of stems after the flowers fall off.

CULTURE. Erodiums are tolerant, adaptable plants, but prefer shade, soil with good drainage, and enough water to keep them on the moist side. Easily propagated by seed or division; set plants 6 inches apart for quick coverage. Hardy to 20°.

USES. Excellent in rock gardens and as a small-scale ground cover. No traffic.

Euonymus
Wintercreeper

The wintercreeper *(E. fortunei)* is an evergreen vine or shrub that makes a very useful ground cover where it is given nothing to climb and allowed to grow flat. Pointed, somewhat leathery, dark green, jagged leaves, 1½ to 2 inches long, are set oppositely along trailing stems which often root where they touch moist soil. Flowers are only occasionally produced, and are inconspicuous. The plant spreads rapidly to about 4 feet while building up to a height of about 2 feet.

Several varieties make better ground covers than the species. The most widely used is purpleleaf wintercreeper *(E. f.* 'Colorata'), characterized by the striking color of its foliage in fall and winter when it turns various hues of purple. It forms a fairly dense carpet 6 to 10 inches high. 'Kew' *(E. f.* 'Kewensis') and baby wintercreeper *(E. f.* 'Minima') are dwarf types, more delicate, slower and lower growing, reaching a height of hardly more than 2 inches. Both retain their small evergreen leaves throughout the year, the leaves of 'Minima' being somewhat larger. Variegated wintercreeper *(E. f.* 'Gracilis') is smaller, less vigorous than 'Colorata' and is notable for its variegated, whitish leaves that take on a pink tinge in winter. The virtues of *E. f.* 'radicans'

Epimedium

Erodium

Duchesnea indica

are that it is the fastest growing of the small-leaved varieties, and its leaves are uniform in size and shape.

CULTURE. Wintercreepers are hardy, sturdy plants that will grow in most parts of the country, in sun or shade, good or poor soil. They are drought resistant but do not do well in hot desert areas even when adequately watered. 'Colorata' tends to get tall but responds well to mowing at an 8-inch height. They can be propagated by division, layering, or cuttings. Divided or rooted plants should be planted in spring, set about 2 feet apart. Euonymus are particularly subject to scale infestation. Euonymus scale causes yellowish or whitish spots on the leaves at first; later leaves drop and branches

die. Control with a dormant oil spray in early spring followed by Orthene or Diazinon sprays when the orange-red crawlers appear. Hardy to —20°.

USES. The dwarf and other small-leaved varieties are not good for large-scale planting, but are highly effective trailing over walls or between rocks or stepping stones. *E. f.* 'Colorata' is excellent for mass planting, particularly on steep hillsides, where it provides good erosion control, or wherever it might serve to cover barren, unsightly places.

Festuca
Blue fescue

Blue fescue *(F. ovina 'glauca')* is an attractive ornamental grass composed of hairlike leaves growing to 4 to 10 inches high in rounded, bluish-gray

tufts. Although a true grass, it is not a practical lawn substitute because of its mounding habit.

CULTURE. Blue fescue is successfully grown in ordinary well-drained soil and full sun. It is drought resistant, but does need regular summer watering. Weeding between tufts can be minimized by the application of a light mulch. Shabby plants can be clipped to remove seed heads, restore appearance, and to stimulate new growth. Start new plants from divisions. It's hardy everywhere, tolerating temperatures to —40°.

USES. When planted in a fairly large area, blue fescue looks best in geometric patterns rather than at random. Two or three plants can provide an effective accent, while

Ferns

Ferns are a natural for producing a cool, woods-like effect. And, despite their delicate appearance, most are very hardy.

Athyrium goeringianum *'Pictum'*

Athyrium goeringianum *'Pictum'*

Dryopteris *(wood fern)*

a row of plants can be a good walk border or edging for a flower bed.

Fragaria
Wild or sand strawberry

A parent of all commercial strawberries, the evergreen *F. chiloensis* forms a highly attractive thick mat of 2-inch dark green leaves that turn a reddish hue in winter. The leaves are oval, roughly toothed on their upper parts, crinkly in texture, and glossy. A profusion of white flowers, 1 inch wide, appears in spring, followed by small, edible fruit. A hybrid known as Hybrid Ornamental Strawberry Number 25, developed and tested in Southern California, is similar but grows more vigorously, is larger in all respects, and produces delicious fruit. 'Baron Solemacher' is a clump-growing strawberry that is often used in the North.

CULTURE. *Fragaria chiloensis* grows in full sun and in most well-drained soils, doing particularly well in sand dunes at the beach. Regular watering is needed throughout the year. Foliage growth is stimulated by light mowing in the spring. New plants are best started from sections of runners planted 12 inches apart. Wild strawberry is subject to infestations of red spider, which can be controlled by spraying twice a year with a combination spray. Hardy to −15°.

USES. Wild strawberry is excellent anywhere in the garden, in beds or as borders, contributing a delightful woodsy effect. It is an ideal ground cover at the beach, particularly on slopes. Accepts light traffic.

Galium
Sweet woodruff

Sweet woodruff (*G. odoratum*) is a beautiful ground cover for shady spots. It grows rapidly, spreading by underground stems into dense, high mats. Tiny, white flowers in the shape of 4-petal crosses bloom from April into summer. They appear in clusters at the end of square, slender stems 6 to 12 inches high covered by long, narrow leaves set in whorls of eight. The leaves have a delicate fragrance suggestive of fresh hay or vanilla.

CULTURE. This is one perennial herb that does best in part or full shade and moist, loamy soil. Most easily propagated by dividing the creeping stems at the beginning of the dormant

Mateuccia struthiopteris

Mateuccia struthiopteris

Adiantium pedatum

winter period. Set out new plants in spring, 8 to 12 inches apart. Self-sows freely once established. May even become a delightful pest. Hardy to —30°.

USES. Provides lovely effect under trees, well-developed rose bushes, rhododendrons and along garden paths. Gives feeling of shady forest. Good bulb cover. Too delicate for traffic. Dried leaves are used in sachets and to flavor wine drinks such as May wine. When steeped in boiling water it becomes a tea. There's a place for sweet woodruff in every garden.

Gaultheria
Wintergreen, teaberry, checkerberry

The herb, *G. procumbens* is the source of the essential oil of wintergreen,

thus its common name. It's hardy (to —35°) and is native to the eastern United States. It is evergreen and usually no higher than 6 inches. Drooping flowers, similar to those of lily-of-the-valley, appear in May and are followed by edible scarlet berries in fall. Leaves are leathery, dark green, and about 1½ inches long. Spreads by underground runners.

CULTURE. Wintergreen needs the same cool, moist environment that promotes the growth of moss. It is easily increased by division of the runner or by whole clumps.

USES. An excellent companion for the taller-growing rhododendrons and azaleas or as a ground cover in native gardens. An excellent ground cover for slope erosion control.

Gelsemium
Carolina jessamine

Popular in gardens as far north as Virginia, *G. sempervirens* has escaped cultivation in many areas. Usually it is evergreen but will lose leaves in winter in cold climates. Most appreciated for its fragrant flowers that appear in early spring. The flowers are yellow, tubular, and about one inch long; leaves are shiny green and finely textured. The state flower of South Carolina. Hardy to about 15°.

CULTURE. It tolerates some shade but flowers more profusely in full sun. Prune selectively and frequently to keep it low (about 3 feet) and to encourage new growth from the base. Almost any soil is suitable but it grows

Grasses and grasslikes

Grass is the most widely used home landscape ground cover, but there are many other forms different from grass used in a conventional lawn.

Festuca ovina 'glauca'

Festuca ovina 'glauca'

Ophiopogon japonicus, *above and right*

best in good loam. Propagate by seeds or cuttings. Not bothered by pests.

USES. Generally best covering large areas, Carolina jessamine is very attractive on a bank or spilling over a retaining wall. Probably more often they are used as a vine, covering a porch, arbor, or trellis.

Genista
Broom

This is a group of shrubs that is so closely related to cytisus they are difficult to distinguish. Genista, like cytisus, is an excellent plant for poor and dry soils, adapted to dry-summer Mediterranean climates. One of the best ground cover species is *G. pilosa.* It has the interesting common name of silky-leaf woadwaxen. Leaves are about ½ inch long and deciduous. In winter the bare twigs remain green. It spreads (forming a clump) up to 7 feet wide and a foot or more high, though usually lower. Yellow pealike flowers appear in May. It is hardy to −10°.

The arrow broom, *G. sagittalis,* is one of the most hardy brooms, tolerating temperatures to −20°. Its branches are bright green in winter and it flowers in June. Height and spread are roughly the same as *G. pilosa* — 1 foot by 7 feet.

CULTURE. Like cytisus, these are plants for hot, dry, sunny situations. They are exceptionally tolerant once established but can be difficult to to transplant. Propagate by cuttings taken in August. See Cytisus for more information.

USES. These are good rock garden and low-maintenance plants that remain obscure most of the year until springtime flowers become eye-catchers.

Glechoma
Ground ivy, gill-over-the-ground

G. hederacea (previously known as *Nepeta hederacea*) is a fairly dense, creeping perennial 3 to 6 inches high. It has attractive, bright green, roundish leaves with scalloped edges and whorled clusters of light blue flowers that bloom in the spring and summer. Grows so vigorously it becomes a pest if not contained. May be more familiar to some as a lawn weed.

Variegated liriope, above and below

Phalaris arundinacea 'Picta'

Liriope

Erica vagans

Erica vagans

Daboecia cantabrica

Daboecia cantabrica

CULTURE. Does equally well in shade or sun in average soil. Needs only periodic summer watering. Propagate by seed or division. Plant 12 inches apart. Very hardy, to —25°.

USES. Once regarded as nothing but a lawn weed, it can be a useful ground cover in limited areas and where it is separate from other plants. Sturdy, but no traffic.

Heaths and heathers

These are special plants loved by many collectors. Enough varieties are available so that mild-climate land-scapes can bloom all year. The heaths and heathers include *Erica* species (heath), *Calluna vulgaris* (true Scotch heather), and *Daboecia* (Irish heath). All plants grow best in similar environments. They are fine-textured and, when in flower, are covered by many small, red to white, bell-shaped flowers.

E. carnea is called either spring or Christmas heath. In mild-winter areas it begins blooming as early as November. More severe winters hold it in check until spring. This is an excellent ground cover, requiring little care once established. It is low, rarely exceeding 1 foot and spreads to 2 to 3 feet (plant on 2½′ centers). The ever-green leaves are less than ¼ inch long and circle the stem in groups of four. Flowers are 1 to 2 inches long and hang down. In cold climates some winter protection may be necessary (hardy to —10°). Spring heath prefers acid soil but does tolerate slight alkalinity. Best flowering is in full sun but in hot-summer areas afternoon shade is advisable. *E. vagans,* bushy and rounded in most varieties, is choice for color and hardiness.

The heathers, *Calluna vulgaris,* are somewhat more hardy (to —20°) and have smaller, overlapping, evergreen leaves that are suggestive of junipers. They also grow taller — some varieties reach 2 feet. Different leaf colors are available too, ranging from solid yellow-gold to the familiar light green. Flowers are minute, about ¼ inch long, and are available in many shades of red and white. Heathers are somewhat slower growing than the heaths so should be planted closer — about 1 foot apart. Use a mulch to control weeds until they establish a cover.

Irish heath *(Daboecia cantabrica)* is an 18-inch shrub that carries slightly drooping, ½-inch flowers on upright stems. Bloom lasts throughout summer beginning in February or May and lasting as late as November. Several varieties of different flower color are available. Leaves are most similar to calluna but are smaller. Use cuttings or division to propagate. The species is lavender, 'Alba' is white, and 'Praegerae' is rose-pink. Irish heath tolerates temperatures to −10°.

CULTURE. The heaths and heathers are tough, low-maintenance plants. Soil must be acidic, moist, and especially well-drained. If soils are too dry or water-logged, add generous amounts of organic matter. Planting in raised beds or mounds also improves drainage. Heaths and heathers stay more compact and flower better in soils that are not too rich. Roots are close to the surface so instead of using a cultivator, apply a mulch to keep the soil loose. In early spring cut back to remove flower stalks and to stimulate dense growth. By pinning a branch to the ground and mounding soil over it (layering), you can easily increase your supply of these plants.

USES. The low-growing heaths and heathers serve very well not only as ground covers but also as borders and edging plants. Deep and tightly woven roots help prevent soil erosion on banks and slopes. They tolerate coastal, salt-laden air and exposed, windy locations. The flowers dry and last many months indoors. They are excellent low-maintenance ground covers requiring almost no attention once established.

Hedera
Ivy

The American Ivy Society President Henri K. E. Schaepman and Communications Director Rona Schaepman write about the large genus Hedera.

When it comes to ground covers, ivy is a natural — so much so that in some places it appears to grow spontaneously. But don't be fooled. Ivy, botanically Hedera, was brought to this country by English settlers. And what a successful import it turned out to be! As a ground cover, ivy does almost everything: stays green the entire year, spreads rapidly, lies flat, climbs and covers, prevents erosion, provides insulation, works in sun or shade, adapts to most climates, requires minimal care, is easily propagated, and — besides all that — can be enormously attractive.

It is no wonder then that this mischievous beauty of a plant excels not only as a well-planned part of the landscape, but also as a container plant, in topiary and bonsai, in terraria and in floral wreaths, as decoration or hanging basket. Ivy is even becoming popular at flower shows, where spectacular specimens have been entered in competition.

But since ivy has been used for centuries mainly as ground cover, it would be well to start there — and to get acquainted with its diversification and the almost endless possibilities of color, shape, size, and application for the landscape.

The photographs on pages 38 and 39 demonstrate some of the landscape uses to which ivy is ideally suited. The ivies shown are cultivars of *Hedera helix,* the species most common in the U.S. and Western Europe, and *H. canariensis,* named for the Canary Islands from which it once was thought to have come; it is commonly known as Algerian ivy.

There are three other species of ivy: *H. colchica* (Persian ivy), *H. nepalensis* (Nepal ivy), and *H. rhombea* (Japanese ivy).

A good comparison of the five species is provided by the first photograph on page 36. Differences in leaf size, shape, and color are readily apparent in the specimen of (left to right): *H. nepalensis, H. helix* (the cultivar 'Welsomi' shown), *H. colchica, H. rhombea,* and *H. canariensis.*

A little familiarity with the typical element of each species makes identification fairly certain. Cultivar identification is more difficult — and far more interesting. The gallery of ivy

Erica carnea

Calluna vulgaris

photographs on pages 36 and 37 shows some of the better known or more distinctive ivy cultivars.

The species *H. helix* has the most cultivars, due mainly to ivy's penchant for sporting — making spontaneous changes in its genetic makeup. In sporting, a plant will suddenly and for no apparent reason produce leaves that differ from the original ones in color, shape, size, growth pattern, or any combination of these. This apparent genetic instability is one reason identification is so challenging, and why it is one of the main concerns of the American Ivy Society.

The second photo on page 36 compares leaf sizes. The familiar *H. h.* 'Hibernica,' commonly called

English Ivy (although *hibernia* is Latin for Irish) is at the top. Its leaves are usually 3 to 3½ inches across. The others shown are classified as miniatures in the system developed by American Ivy Society founder Suzanne Pierot, which assembles *helix* cultivars by leaf shape. Immediately below 'Hibernica' is 'Midget,' and below that the variegated 'Jubilee' (an outstanding hanging basket plant). To the right is the self-branching 'La Plata,' and to the left 'Pixie.'

The habit known as self-branching is shown in the third photo, where 'Cascade' (right) sprouts a tuft of leaves from every axillary bud, whereas 'Crenata' is an example of a regular, not ramose, ivy. 'Baltica'

competes for first place among ground covers with 'Hibernica.' When the two are compared, 'Baltica' has smaller leaves, slightly darker green color, and more prominent veins. It is acclaimed as one of the hardiest ivies.

'Pittsburgh' (also known as 'Hahn Self-branching') does well when used as ground cover. It is a little lighter green than the others. These cultivars of typical ivy leaf shape fall into the ivy-ivies classification.

Next are the fans, beginning with the compact, bright rich green *H.h.* 'Fan.' 'California Fan' has leaves broader than long; it grows compactly and makes a good ground cover. 'Green Ripple' is glossy dark green, of pleasing appearance.

Hedera — Ivy

Diverse in both beauty and function, a gallery of ivies photographed against the same background displays variations in leaf size, color, and shape.

(see page 35 for identification) (see page 35 for identification) H. helix *Crenata,* *Cascade* H.h. *Baltica*

H.h. *Irish Lace* H.h. *Needlepoint* H.h. *Imp* H.h. *Dragonclaw* H.h. *Ivalace*

H.h. *Sagittaefolia variegata* H.h. *Sulphurea* H.h. *Fantasia* H.h. *California Gold* H.h. *Buttercup*

'Green Feather' is a bird's-foot, belonging to a group whose leaves appear to fit the tracks left by a bird walking in the snow. This cultivar grows close and compact (compare the number of leaves shown with the leaves of 'Green Ripple'). The lateral lobes are folded over the main lobe, giving 'Green Feather' a pointed appearance. 'Irish Lace' is a more pronounced, scraggly bird's-foot.

''Needlepoint' is a name used for several different cultivars. The correctly named plant (shown) is a self-branching dwarf. The final bird's-foot here is the mostly unlobed 'Imp.'

The curlies are illustrated, first, by 'Dragonclaw,' a frilly specimen whose large leaves curl downward. 'Ivalace,' a shiny, leathery-leaved, self-branching curly is distinctive — a good ground cover.

'Deltoidea' is a heartshaped ivy. Leaves are dull, dark green, veins greenish-gray. 'Tomboy' leaves are shiny and more pointed.

The variegateds remain — a term that includes specimen whose leaves differ in color from the all-green plant. 'Glacier' has come to refer to any ivy that has marginal white variegation. Actually, 'Glacier' leaves come in several shades of green, white, and gray, all small, triangular, and leathery, with white margins.

'Herold' leaves are large and beautiful, with silver variegation. 'Eva' is small, with silver variegation. 'Sagittifolia variegata' is a gorgeous plant, with creamy white edging. It is much in demand, but very tender.

'Sulphurea' has variegation that almost defies description. It is not limited to the margins, nor is the leaf speckled. The leaf appears delicate yet strong and beautifully shaped (curving, somewhat convex).

'Fantasia' is speckled white; 'California Gold,' heavily self-branching and bushy, has gold specks. 'Buttercup' leaves are not speckled but uniformly butter yellow when young. They are attractive and seem to glow from within.

'Gold Heart' is just that: a small green leaf with a heart of gold (or cream). It is familiar and popular,

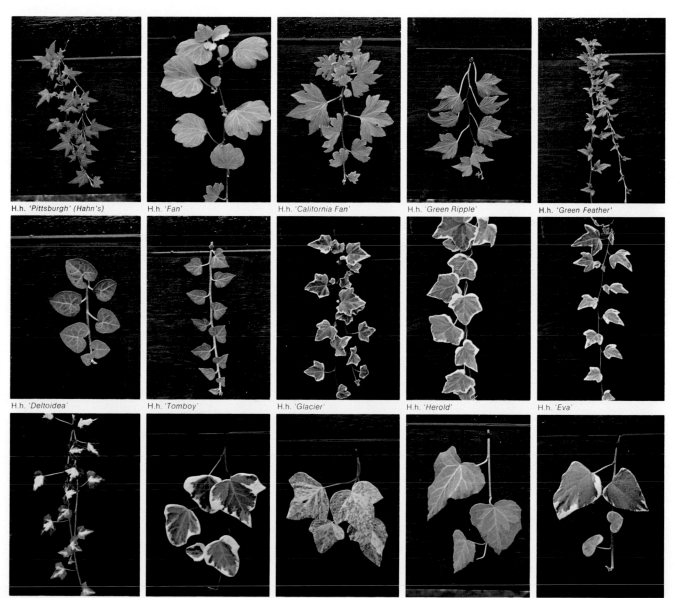

H.h. 'Pittsburgh' (Hahn's)   H.h. 'Fan'   H.h. 'California Fan'   H.h. 'Green Ripple'   H.h. 'Green Feather'

H.h. 'Deltoidea'   H.h. 'Tomboy'   H.h. 'Glacier'   H.h. 'Herold'   H.h. 'Eva'

H.h. 'Gold Heart'   H. canariensis 'Variegata'   H.can. 'Aureo-maculata'   H. colchica 'Sulphur Heart'   H.col. 'Dentato-variegata' but requires selective pruning when grown as ground cover.

Next are cultivars of the species *H. canariensis* — both examples are large-leaved and variegated, the first marginally, the second speckled.

H. colchica cultivars are always leathery — even when variegated. The last four photographs on page 37 show that different kinds of variegation are not solely an attribute of *H. helix* cultivars.

CULTURE. It is easy to grow ivies with spectacular success if the plant's cultural likes and dislikes are taken into account.

An ivy bed is most easily begun with well-established plants, which can be purchased in pots. Fast-growing cultivars should be planted one per square foot; small-leaved or slow-growing ivies, four to the square foot, or you may find two or three the ideal. Generally, self-branching and compact growers will cover more densely.

Ivy requires a well-draining soil and, contrary to popular belief, it needs a high light intensity. It grows best in indirect light, but once established will tolerate full sun or even fairly heavy shade. In deep shade, however, ivy will merely survive — it will not thrive.

After the initial growth — ivy spurts in spring and, especially, in fall — you can replenish or extend your ivies by taking cuttings. Ivies will grow well despite adverse conditions. They root easily — even in water. It is best to make two-node cuttings (always of healthy, typical leaves), and place them in well-moistened flat of Jiffy Mix or other propagating soil. Cuttings should be stuck very shallow: the deeper you stick them into the propagating medium, the more likely they will rot. Give cuttings indirect light until they root, and keep the leaves moist.

Maintenance of the ivy bed is easy. It is a good practice to mow it every other year (just prior to new growth), with the mower at the highest setting. This prevents the growth from becoming so dense it can harbor undesirable animal life. The plants will be covered with leaves with the first growth of spring.

Hedera — Ivy

Ivy is one of the most versatile and reliable plants in the ground cover world — growing anywhere from steep slopes to shade.

Hedera helix *'Baltica'*

Hedera canariensis

Hedera helix *'Baltica'*

A habit peculiar to many ivy cultivars is that of reversion. This is simply sporting in reverse. For example, a variegated-type ivy starts putting out all-green shoots. Almost all cultivars will sport-revert on occasion. Although some cultivars are quite stable, others must be selectively pruned frequently. To preserve the desirable qualities, the grower must cut the nonconforming twig back to a leaf with the desired characteristics; a new, normal shoot will develop from the axillary bud.

USES. For outside planting, it is best to use the more stable cultivars. Indoors, the most beautiful ivies often turn out to be the least stable. This is one reason it is important to buy col-lectors' items from a reputable grower who keeps his propagating stock pure by constant and painstaking selection. He is also likely to be more precise in naming his ivies.

Outdoors the grower must be on the watch for leaf spot, which begins as one-quarter-inch brown or black spots. This is generally not serious, but it can become unsightly. If it does, spray the area with a fungicide containing copper.

The grower should also be aware of his climate so he may choose his cultivars for ground cover intelligently. In hot, dry regions care will include watering the ivy beds — much as you would water a lawn. In colder areas you must consider the exposure of the plants: a combination of winter sun and frozen soil will result in frost damage. Exposure to a drying winter wind will have the same result; use Wiltpruf or a similar product to alleviate this.

Indoors, the greatest enemy of ivy is red spider mite. Since mites like it hot and dry, and ivy prefers an environment cool and moist, there is a ready preventive for this pest: just give ivy what it likes. If this is impossible, or mites appear anyway, launder your plants. A brisk shower and mild soap does wonders — and you might make this a weekly practice even before you see the pests.

There are too many factors involved to predict which cultivars are suitable for a particular area. It is best to con-

Hedera helix *'Hibernica'*

Hedera helix *'Lobato-major'*

Hedera helix *'Hibernica'*

sult local garden centers or specialists, or write the American Ivy Society.

Founded in 1971, the AIS Research Center grows most *Hedera* cultivars. Its director and current AIS President, Henri K. E. Schaepman, has compiled more than 400 specimen descriptions and histories in a *Preliminary Checklist.* AIS Communications Director, Rona Schaepman, edits a quarterly *Bulletin* that tells members all about ivy and its place in horticulture. Membership is $7.50 annually for the *Bulletin,* special offers, and everything you ever wanted to know about ivy. Pierot's *The Ivy Book* (Macmillan, 1974) is $6.50, and the *Checklist* is $5 for postage and printing costs (both prepaid). Inquiries are welcome:

American Ivy Society, National Center for American Horticulture, Mt. Vernon, VA 22121.

When they can't give you a specific answer — or even when they can — the Society will encourage you to experiment on your own. Ivy is just too much fun to miss.

Helianthemum
Sun rose

H. nummularium is a hardy, evergreen, spreading plant that makes an excellent ground cover, particularly if a low-maintenance garden is desired. A vigorous, long-lived native of the Mediterranean region, it is adapted to dry summers. Height is usually 6 to 8 inches though some reach

1 foot. Each plant ultimately forms a clump about 3 feet in diameter. Branches root as they spread, eventually creating a thick mat. Leaves are narrow, growing to 1 inch in length. Depending on the variety, they are glossy or dull green. Bright, 1- to 2-inch flowers are single or double, and are available in shades of pink, red, or yellow. The blossoms are delicate and last only a day, but enough flowers on a plant open over a long period that their short life goes unnoticed. Hardy to —20°.

CULTURE. Sun roses need full sun and neutral-to-alkaline soil. To grow them in high rainfall-acid soil areas, amend the soil with lime before planting. Otherwise they are very unde-

Hemerocallis — Daylily

Daylilies are equally attractive when viewed close-up as below, or, when grouped in a mass, as in the landscaping scenes opposite. Hemerocallis means "beautiful for the day."

'Call to Remember'

'Cherub'

'Doxology'

'Florence Byrd'

'King of Glory'

'Knee Baby'

'Pink Devotion'

'Sail On'

'Tamiko'

manding, growing better in relatively dry, unfertile soil. They can adapt to wet areas if the drainage is excellent. Shear in spring after first flowering to stimulate growth for late summer bloom and to keep the plants dense and compact. They can be difficult to transplant — purchase rooted cuttings if possible and plant 12 to 18 inches apart. They rarely tolerate root disturbance, once they are established. Where winters are cold and there is no snow cover, insulate with straw or similar material to protect from dessicating winter winds. Propagate with cuttings from new spring growth (late June) or by division.

USES. Sun roses do very well in rock gardens — cascading over and around rocks or tucked into pockets. A close relative of the rock roses (cistus), they also have fire-retardant properties.

Hemerocallis
Daylily

There aren't many plants as tough and pest-free as the daylilies. They grow in nearly any soil or climate and fit into the landscape in many ways. Insects and diseases leave them alone. On top of it all they offer spectacular and fragrant flowers. If you choose varieties carefully, you can manage to have daylilies in flower from May to October in the mildest climates, perhaps a month or so less in cold regions. Some are repeat bloomers; some bloom in the evening.

The color range runs from the original yellow, orange, rust, and red, to hybrids in pink, vermilion, buff, apricot, white, and two-colored varieties. The flower size runs from 3 to 8 inches, and the range of height begins with the 12-inch dwarfs and goes on to 6 feet. There are both evergreen kinds for warm climates, and deciduous kinds that will grow nearly anywhere. They are excellent for naturalizing your landscape.

Daylilies are a collector's plant. If you are interested in learning more about them, contact the American Hemerocallis Society, Signal Mountain, Tennessee 37377. For your $5 dues, they send a quarterly publication.

A mass planting, a doorway accent, a flowerbed corner — all benefit from the beauty of hemerocallis.

CULTURE: Daylilies can be moved any time of year but the best time is in spring. Plant them on 2-foot centers in a good, well-drained soil. Their need for water is not great but applying plenty before and during bloom will insure the best flowering. As for fertilizer, apply a balanced type in spring and early summer.

It is possible to leave daylilies in place indefinitely without attention, but they will perform better if divided every 4 to 6 years. This increases your supply of plants and provides some to share. Dig the entire clump in early spring or late fall. Fall is preferable with deciduous varieties since you'll find them more easily than if you wait until they're completely dormant. Using two spading forks, plunge the tines of both into the center of the clump, then pull the handles to pry the clump in two (or three, or four). Replant with the top of the fleshy roots at soil level.

USES. The uses of daylilies are varied. Some, like *H. fulva* 'Europa,' are so tough they can reclaim poor or damaged soil, grow by railroad tracks, or hold river banks. Another tough daylily is *H. fulva* 'Kwanso.' It's often used along country lanes to naturalize.

Daylilies are also edible after dipping the fresh flower buds in egg batter and deep-frying them.

Daylilies make excellent cut flowers. Choose a stem with several ready-to-bloom buds. In the home they'll open, one per day, lasting only a day. Translated from the Greek, hemerocallis means "beautiful for the day."

Herbs

Botanically, an herb is a nonwoody plant. In more popular usage, an herb is a plant that is valued for some culinary, cosmetic, or medicinal purpose.

This latter definition not only includes a lot of plants, it leads to the arbitrary inclusion of many non-herbaceous plants, (lavender and rosemary, for example). We are not making this distinction to quibble but only to put the category "herbs" in clearer perspective. Now, why are we proposing the use of herbs, using the

Herbs

Fragrant and kitchen-functional — two more reasons to grow herbs as ground covers. Here are some favorites.

Galium odoratum

Thymus

Thymus *(woolly thyme)*

popular definition, as ground covers? Simply, because they offer numerous rewards. They show different, interesting textures and patterns, provide fragrance and color and are generally easy to grow. Herbs are sturdy and hardy with regard to temperature. The two basic horticultural requirements for most herbs are a light, well-drained soil and full sun.

Limitations? Most herbs are for looking at, not for walking on; they are usually either too delicate or too tall for traffic.

The following is a list of those herbs that are star performers as ground covers. To find out about an herb in detail, refer to them in this chapter alphabetically.

Achillea tomentosa. Woolly yarrow
Anthemis nobilis. Chamomile
Artemisia. Wormwood
Galium odoratum. Sweet woodruff
Gaultheria. Wintergreen
Lavandula angustifolia.
English lavender
Mentha requienii. Corsican mint
Nepeta mussinii. Catmint
Rosmarinus officinalis 'Prostratus.'
Prostrate rosemary
Santolina chamaecyparissus.
Lavender cotton
Stachys byzantina. Lamb's ears
Teucrium chamaedrys
Dwarf germander
Thymus. Thyme

Herniaria
Rupturewort

Rupturewort *(H. glabra)* is a trailing herb that forms a dense, glossy green carpet 2 to 4 inches high. In warm climates, it is grown as an evergreen perennial; in cool areas, foliage turns bronzy-red in winter; in cold areas, it is treated as an annual. The plant grows slowly, spreading by rooting stems.
CULTURE. Grows in sun or light shade and in most well-drained soils. Needs regular watering. Propagate by division, setting out divided plants 6 to 8 inches apart. Hardy to —20°.
USES. Ideal between stepping stones, particularly red brick pavers. Takes light traffic.

Lavender, above and below right.

Corsican mint

Dwarf rosemary

Heuchera
Coralbells

Coralbells *(H. sanguinea)* are ever-green perennials popular throughout the country. Not a large-scale ground cover but well suited for brightening small spots. Flowers are bell-shaped, either coral-pink or red, about ½ inch long. They are borne on 2-foot stalks that appear first in June and last until September. In mild-winter areas, they may bloom all year. Evergreen leaves are roundish, tinged red in winter. Roots are long and fleshy. There are many selections available usually varying by flower color. Hardy to —35°.

CULTURE. Coralbells have few problems and can usually be left to take care of themselves for extended periods of time. Soil should be well-drained and moist. Some shade is best, with protection provided from hot afternoon sun. Plant 1 foot apart in spring in cold areas (protect with a mulch in winter); plant anytime elsewhere. Don't plant too deep — crowns may rot. To propagate, divide clumps or take a leaf cutting with a small portion of the stem attached. Plants need to be divided when they become woody and produce few flowers. Extend flowering period by removing faded flowers.

USES. Coralbells are good edging plants for perennial borders in which roses, delphiniums, peonies, and similar plants grow. They are favored plants of hummingbirds, and are attractive as cut flowers.

Hosta
Plantain lilies, funkia

The plantain lilies are a large and valuable group of deciduous perennials valued mainly for their dramatic foliage. They're hardy, long-lived, and one of the best plants to grow in shade. All varieties are deciduous — they die to the ground each winter and are renewed each spring.

Hosta

Hosta

Hosta

Heuchera sanguinea

Hypericum *blossom*

Hypericum calycinum

The blunt plantain lily *(H. decorata)* has oval leaves about 6 inches long. The tips are blunt or abruptly pointed and 8 to 10 parallel veins are prominent. Two-inch-long bell-shaped flowers are dark blue-purple, appearing in summer on thin stalks. The variety 'Royal Standard' is slightly taller and has long-stemmed flowers.

The narrow-leaved plantain lily *(H. lancifolia)* is one of the lower-growing plantain lilies. Leaves are narrow, shorter (4 inches) and pointed. Flowers, occurring in summer, are a light shade of blue-purple.

Fragrant plantain lily *(H. plantaginea)* has large, 10-inch leaves and large flowers (4-5 inches) that are known for their fragrance. They appear in late summer or early fall.

The most impressive leaves belong to *H. sieboldiana.* They are blue-green, 10-15 inches long, and are heavily veined. Flowers are much less significant — they're small (1½ inches long) and on stalks usually shorter than the leaves. This hosta makes a dramatic accent by a shaded pool. Several varieties of this species are grown. Leaves of 'Frances Williams' have yellow-cream borders.

Wavy-leaved plantain lily *(H. undulata)* makes taller mounds (to 3 feet) than most types. It also tolerates more sun. It is popular for its 6-inch, variegated, wavy leaves, often used in floral arrangements. Pale lavender, 2-inch flowers appear in spring on 3-foot stalks.

A hybrid plantain lily named 'Honeybells' has the most outstanding flowers of the group. They bloom late on 3-foot stalks and are more open, much like Easter lilies. The dull lavender-lilac blossoms are also very fragrant.

CULTURE. Hostas are easy to grow. They prefer a sandy or loamy soil, high in organic matter, that has good drainage. Medium to dense shade is a necessity.

Bait for snails and slugs, who love the leaves. Plantain lilies are very hardy (to about −30°). *H. decorata* is somewhat less hardy, tolerating temperatures only to −10°. Hostas perform best in cold-winter areas.

USES. Plantain lilies are excellent border plants and have long been used to edge perennial beds or shrubs. Where shade is too heavy, as it can be under trees or facing a northern exposure, plantain lilies are of great practical value. Planted singly as accent plants, plantain lilies break up the monotony of too many smaller-leaved plants.

Hypericum
Aaron's beard, St. John's-wort

Widely regarded as one of the best ground covers available, *H. calycinum* is a handsome plant and is easy to grow. Foliage is evergreen except in cold-area winters where it becomes dormant. Leaves are oblong, 2 to 3 inches in length, and bright green. The flowers, about 3½ inches across, have pale yellow petals with delicate tufts of orange-yellow stamens rising from the center. They bloom through most of the summer, appearing singly

and scattered throughout a planting. This sturdy species grows rapidly to a height of 12-15 inches and spreads freely by underground shoots.

CULTURE. Grows equally well in sun or part shade, sandy or loamy soils. The plant survives drought, but needs plenty of water to look its best. Propagate by seed, or more easily by division, setting plants 12 to 18 inches apart. Shear tops each spring to rejuvenate and keep compact.

USES. This is a dense ground cover, excellent for mass planting. Because of its strong root system it offers erosion control on slopes; it can also be invasive unless confined. Using a header board or other divider will contain the plants, which also helps to keep the planting trim.

Iberis
Evergreen candytuft

Evergreen candytuft *(I. sempervirens)* is an attractive 6- to 12-inch high ground cover covered with white, flat flower clusters in early spring. The clusters, about 2 inches across, appear at the top of stems heavily set with narrow, dark green leaves 1½ inches long. The foliage forms a

Ilex vomitoria *'Nana'*

Iberis sempervirens

Ilex crenata *'Helleri'* with I. cornuta *'Rotunda'*

Ilex cornuta *'Carissa'*

dense mat as the long stems bend to the ground and root again. Several varieties are more compact. Among them are 'Snowflake,' which grows to about 9 inches, 'Little Gem,' about 6 inches high, and 'Little Cushion,' also about 6 inches high and spreading a foot or more.

CULTURE. Candytuft grows best in a good, well-drained soil and in full sun. It needs regular watering throughout the year. Propagation is easy by seed, cuttings, or division. Old flowers should be cut away to encourage new growth.

USES. Candytuft is handsome anywhere in the garden. It makes a good edging for walks and can also be used as a general, small-scale cover. Try using it in a rock garden or let it spill gracefully over a wall. The stems of the flowers are long enough to make bouquets. Hardy (to −20°) throughout most of the country.

Ilex
Holly

The hollies are highly ornamental trees or shrubs notable for their shiny green, leathery leaves and clusters of mostly red (sometimes yellow or black) berries. Some are self-fertile and others need both a male and female plant to produce berries.

Dwarf varieties of the species listed here, all of them evergreen, are suitable for use as ground covers.

They range from 1 to 3 feet in height. A number of varieties of English holly (I. aquifolium) have variegated leaves. One of the best is 'Golden Queen,' distinguished by its sharply pointed, somewhat crinkly yellow and green leaves. Despite its name, it is a male plant and produces no berries.

Five low-growing varieties of Chinese holly (I. cornuta), developed by Monrovia nursery of Southern California, are:

'Berries Jubilee' — slow growing, compact, mounding habit; large bright red berries in profusion; large, spatula-shaped leaves. A handsome plant.

'Burfordi Nana' ('Dwarf Burford') — a dwarf version of the Burford holly

Juniperus—Juniper

Junipers could be described as the essence of ground cover plants — hardy, evergreen, and easy to maintain, with a large selection to fit any garden. Our gallery of juniper standouts should make the selection chore easier.

J. chinensis 'Fruitlandi'   J.c. 'San Jose'   J.c. aurea 'Gold Coast'   J.c. sargenti 'Glauca'

J. horizontalis 'Bar Harbor'   J.h. 'Blue Chip'   J.h. 'Emerald Spreader'   J.h. 'Hughes'

J. sabina 'Arcadia'   J.s. 'Broadmoor'   J.s. 'Buffalo'   J.s. 'New Name'

characterized by smooth-edged leaves, slow growth, and copious production of bright red berries.

'Carissa' — slow growing, dense, mounding foliage.

'Dazzler' — large clusters of large red berries and leaves similar to 'Berries Jubilee' but a lighter green.

I.c. 'Rotunda' — dwarf Chinese holly. Medium growth rate, no berries. Japanese holly *(Ilex crenata)* is characterized by small, dark green leaves about 1 inch long, dense foliage, compact form, and small blue-black berries of insignificant ornamental value. Three useful varieties of *I. crenata* are:

'Compacta' — compact and dense, very small leaves about ½ inch long.

'Green Island' — more open in form, a mature plant grows to 3 feet high, 6 feet across.

'Helleri' — one of the original dwarf varieties. Small leaves, very compact, about the same height and spread of 'Green Island.'

Two of the lowest-growing hollies are varieties of yaupon *(I. vomitoria).* They are: 'Nana' — a dwarf yaupon having thickly set, narrow, dark green leaves to 1 inch long and producing quantities of tiny red berries. This compact plant grows to about 1½ feet high, 3 to 4 feet wide.

'Stokes' — similar to 'Nana' but lower growing.

CULTURE. These hollies thrive in a good, well-drained garden soil in full sun or light shade. Regular watering is needed throughout the year. They can be pruned to shape and control growth. Holly leaf miner is the most serious insect pest. Spray Orthene or Diazinon when damage is first noticed. Mealybug, white fly, and scale are occasionally pests and are easily controlled. See page 89. Japanese holly is the hardiest of the species listed here, but all can be considered hardy to −5°.

USES. One or two plants together provide a striking accent anywhere in the landscape that conditions permit. When spaced a foot or less apart, they make excellent edgings along walks or adjacent to low stone walls. Planted closer together,

J.c. sargenti *'Viridis'*   J. procumbens *'Nana'*   J.p. variegata *'Golden'*   J. squamata expansa *'Parsonii'*

J.h. *'Turquoise Spreader'*   J.h. *Wiltonii*   J.h. *'Yukon Belle'*   J.h. plumosa compacta *'Youngstown'*

J.s. *'Scandia'*   J.s. *'Tamariscifolia'*   J.s. *Tamariscifolia 'New Blue'*   J. virginiana prostrata *'Silver Spreader'*

they make fine hedges that can be trimmed to give a more formal look. The berries are poisonous.

Indigofera
White Chinese indigo

Indigo *(I. incarnata* 'Alba'.) is a low (1½-foot) deciduous shrub. A member of the legume family, it develops a strong root system from which tops are renewed each spring. Roots are hardy to —10° and in mild climates the plant remains evergreen. Leaves are divided into many leaflets each 1 to 3 inches long. Flowers are white, like small sweet peas, and appear in midsummer.

The species *I. kirilowii*, 'Kirilow Indigo,' is taller (to 3 feet) and hardier (to —20°). But it does not become as dense af *I. incarnata* 'Alba' *so is less desirable as a ground cover.*

CULTURE: Indigo grows vigorously and requires no extraordinary care. Plant in full sun. Cut back dead tops (with mower) if they have been winterkilled. In mild climates, pruning back promotes best flowering and most compact growth. Propagate by seeds, cuttings, and division.

USES. The strong interlocking roots of indigo make it a good choice for erosion control on slopes and banks. It's best in large areas. Related species were formerly used as a source of indigo (deep violet-blue) dye.

Iris
Crested iris

I. crisata is native to Maryland, south to Georgia, and west to Missouri. Related to the familiar bearded iris, it forms a thick mat of slender, greenish rhizomes on the surface of the soil. The leaves last until fall and are 4 to 7 inches long, ½ inch wide. In May and June lilac-purple flowers are profuse. The selection 'Alba' has white flowers and 'Caerulea' has blue flowers. Hardy to —30°.

CULTURE. This iris is easily grown, preferring cool, moist soil. It will take full sun but does best with some shade. Accepts acidic soil. To progate, divide after bloom or in fall

Juniperus— Juniper

For a low-maintenance evergreen garden, junipers are a natural choice.

Juniperus conferta

Juniperus *'Marcellus'* above, J.'Tamariscifolia,' *below*

before leaves are gone. The rhizome will rot if covered with soil; bury only the roots when planting.

USES. Plant the crested iris where the rhizomes can creep into cracks and crevices, such as around stones or walkways. They are also effective planted in masses.

Sword-shaped leaves are an effective contrast to smaller-leaved plants.

Juniperus
Junipers

Few ground covers have as many desirable qualities as the prostrate junipers. They are evergreen, sturdy, and require very little maintenance. They are a difficult-to-resist planting choice, even where other plants might do just as well.

The San Jose juniper (*J. chinensis* 'San Jose') is an excellent, sturdy, semiprostrate juniper with upward-spreading branches to 12 inches high and 6 feet across. The foliage is compact and sage-green. This juniper can be used effectively on steep slopes as well as flat areas.

The form *J.c. sargentii* 'Glauca' grows into a low mat 8 to 10 feet across, 10 inches high. Small, scale-like, somewhat feathery foliage is a distinctive blue-green. Native to coastal Japan, it is often used in coastal areas. *J.c. sargentii* 'Viridis' is the same form with rich green foliage. All of these forms of junipers are hardy to —25°.

The form *J. communis saxatilis* is a prostrate juniper with upward spreading branchlets to 1 foot high, 6 feet across. Gray-green foliage is composed of prickly clusters of tiny needle-leaves. It's hardy to —25°.

The shore juniper, *J. conferta* 'Blue Pacific' is a handsome low creeper native to coastal areas of Japan. It has compact, blue-green, somewhat prickly foliage. One plant grows to 10 feet wide and about 10 inches high. An obvious choice for coastal areas and sandy soils, it can also be successfully grown inland given enough water. It looks particularly attractive when allowed to cascade over low stone or cement walls. This plant is somewhat less cold tolerant.

J. chinensis 'Aureo-Pfitzerana'

J. horizontalis

J. chinensis 'Pfitzerana Glauca' (above), J. sabina 'Buffalo' (below).

Lamium maculatum

Indigofera incarnata *'Alba'*

The creeping juniper *(J. horizontalis)* is commonly available in many forms. Here are brief descriptions of the more popular varieties.

'Blue Chip' is a low, mounding juniper with scale-like, silver-blue foliage. It grows about 8 inches high and spreads about 2 feet. This variety makes a very effective border. It's hardy to −25°.

'Bar Harbor' is a juniper of striking architectural character. Its flat branching growth habit is distinctive and the strong gray-green, not-too-dense featherly foliage allows some of the main stems to show through. This variety is very effective planted among large, low rocks. In winter, foliage turns to a silvery plum color. This juniper tolerates temperatures as low as −35°.

'Emerson's Creeper' is a moderately dense, low-branching creeper to about 8 inches high and 6 to 8 feet wide. Scale-like foliage is gray-green. It's hardy to −25°.

'Emerald Spreader' has a more delicate appearance than most. Foliage is feathery, emerald-green,

and lightly branched. It grows to about 10 inches high, spreading 4 to 6 feet. Hardy to −25°.

'Turquoise Spreader' differs from 'Emerald Spreader' in only two characteristics: foliage is more dense and has a bluish cast.

'Hughes' is a vigorous, widely spreading juniper with upward-turning branches to 15 inches high. Gray-green leaves have a bluish cast and are somewhat needle-like. It tolerates cold to −35°.

'Douglasii', the Waukegan juniper, is a sturdy ground cover with a semi-erect trailing habit and bluish-green, scale-like foliage that has a slight purplish hue in winter. Mature height is 12 to 16 inches; it spreads 10 feet. It is used like 'Bar Harbor' but is more hardy, to −35°.

'Plumosa Compacta' is a more compact form of the Andorra juniper *(J. horizontalis* 'Plumosa'). It's similar to 'Douglasii' but has smaller, more feathery, bluish-green leaves that turn purple in the winter. Branchlets are more upright, reaching 10 to 12 inches, and its spread is less, 2 to 4 feet. It is equally hardy, to −35°.

'Wiltonii', the Wilton carpet juniper, is the lowest and probably slowest growing of all ground cover junipers. A spread of 3 feet after 6 years of growth is typical. Also called 'Blue Rug,' its trailing, creeping habit and dense, feathery, silver-blue foliage forms a 4-inch mat. Use on banks or trailing over walls. Cold tolerance is to −25°.

The dwarf Japanese garden juniper, popularly sold as *J. procumbens* 'Nana,' is known botanically as *J. chinensis procumbens* 'Nana.' It's a low-growing, prostrate juniper native to Japan. Foliage is bluish-green, dense, and somewhat prickly. Growth habit is creeping; height builds up to about 6 inches. A good rock garden juniper.

Another selection, 'Variegata,' is the same except for a higher, slightly mounding habit, and gray-green foliage with patches of light yellow. Both varieties are hardy to −25°.

The savin juniper *(J. sabina)* is available in several good ground cover forms.

J. s. 'Broadmoor' grows compactly

to one foot. Leaves are tiny, scale-like, green, and prickly. *J.s.* 'Buffalo' is widely spreading, soft, and feathery. Bright green foliage gives this juniper a striking appearance. Height is 10 to 12 inches and spread is 4 to 6 feet.

J.s. 'Arcadia' is more shrublike than most junipers considered ground covers. Foliage is rich green and lacy. Upward-rising branches spread to 4 feet and reach a height of 20 inches. Excellent for spot planting.

J.s. 'Blue Danube', a native of Austria, has lacy, blue-green foliage. Branches grow upward to about 1 foot and spread 4 feet. Use it either as a ground cover or low shrub.

J.s. 'Scandia' is a rugged, hardy juniper with graceful, spreading branches (to 3 feet) and dense, lacy, yellow-green foliage. Height is about 1 foot. As a mass planting, makes an excellent ground cover.

J.s. 'Tamariscifolia' is the well-known tamarix, or simply "tam," juniper. Arching branches carry dense, lacy, blue-green foliage suggestive of delicate reef coral. It has a mounding (to 20 inches), symmetrical growth habit; spread is to 4 feet. Widely used on slopes, set among rocks, and as a mass planting. The tamarix juniper is the least hardy of this group (to −15°). Others tolerate −25°.

J. squamata expansa 'Parsonii' is a handsome, low-growing, densely branched juniper with relatively thick, gray-green, scale-like leaves. It grows 6 to 10 inches high and spreads 4 to 6 feet. It's hardy to −25°.

J. virginiana prostrata 'Silver Spreader' is a low-growing form of the red cedar tree. Foliage is silvery green and feathery. Branches are upward-spreading to 4 to 6 feet at a height of 20 inches. This a good juniper for accent planting.

CULTURE. Growing ground cover junipers successfully can be narrowed down to three elements: good drainage, full sun, and proper spacing. Attempting to grow junipers in heavy, slow-draining soil often ends in disappointment. Where clay or other heavy soil is prevalent, it should be amended (see page 86).

Junipers need full sun. Some shade is tolerated, but they become woody and lose color. Extra care should be taken in spacing junipers — they are often placed too close together. They are slow growers, but a plant that looks harmlessly small in a one-gallon container can ultimately spread 10 feet in each direction. The tendency to plant more than is necessary is hard to resist. If fast coverage is important, be prepared to remove plants at a later date to avoid crowding.

Despite their sturdy constitution, insects can be troublesome for junipers. A dry, faded look with patchy brown spots on the top of the plant suggests an infestation of spider mites. Minute spiders, large populations of them, drain the plant's vigor. A growing-season oil spray combined with an insecticide such as Malathion will control these pests. A similar treatment is also effective against scale insects such as pine needle scale and juniper scale.

Lamium
Spotted dead nettle

White or yellow splotches along the leaf midrib are the most significant feature of *L. maculatum*. It grows to 6 or 8 inches and the leaves are 1½ inches long. At any time from spring to early summer, purple flowers appear. In fall, leaves become pink to purple. Fast growing and roots as it spreads. The selection 'Aureum' has leaves splotched with yellow. Another species, *L. galeob-dolon* (also known as *Lamiastrum galeobdolon*) has yellow flower spikes and silvery marked leaves and is commonly known as yellow archangel. These plants are hardy (to −20°) but lose their leaves in the coldest winters.

CULTURE. Lamiums prefer shady spots but tolerate full sun if the soil holds enough water. Once established, little attention is required. Propagate by division or seed.

USES. The colorful leaves of these plants make them useful for highlighting shaded or quiet corners and for contrasting with the solid green leaves of surrounding plants.

Lavandula
English lavender

English lavender *(L. angustifolia)* has been cultivated for centuries as an ornamental herb and for its aromatic oil. Recently, dwarf varieties have been developed that, in addition to their delightful fragrance, make attractive ground covers. These varieties have characteristics in common: lance-shaped, green-gray leaves 1 to 2 inches long; ½-inch-wide, blue

Lamium maculatum *with hostas.*

Lobularia maritima

to purple flowers in spikes on long stems 8 inches to 2 feet tall and a moderate growth rate. They grow in clumps 1 to 2 feet wide and bloom about two months in midsummer.

Here are several lavender varieties. See if any of their specialized attributes appeals to you.

'Alba'; identified by white flowers.

'Carrol Gardens'; pale purple flowers.

'Compacta'; compact habit to 8 inches high.

'Dutch'; deep blue flowers.

'Fragrance'; heavily scented.

'Hidcote'; deep purple flowers, 12 inches high.

'Munstead'; lilac-blue flowers, early blooming.

'Twickel Purple'; dark purple flowers in fanlike clusters.

CULTURE. English lavender needs only full sun and average, but well-drained soil to thrive. It can be propagated by seed or division, or by rooting 2- to 5-inch cuttings or new shoots. Set rooted plants 2 feet apart. Established plants can be sheared in early spring to induce dense growth, but after three to four years plants get leggy and the best thing to

Lobularia maritima

do is to take them out and replant. Lavender will take a minimum of —10 to —15°.

USES: As ground cover, English lavender is an excellent choice. It is a natural for borders, and in rock and herb gardens. Beyond these uses, all varieties provide delightful cut flowers.

Our herb gardener reports: "To make a lavender sachet, collect and dry the flower heads just as the flowers start to open. Though not as potent, leaves and stems contain the fragrance and can also be used. The fragrance is very subtle so use at least ⅓ of a cup. If the odor becomes too faint, simply crush the sachet in your hand to release it again. Use lavender to scent sheets, pillows, towels, even stationery."

Lippia (Phyla)

Lippia canescens is a perennial ever-green herb. With some exceptions it makes an excellent lawn substitute in warm climates. It forms a dense mat 1 to 2 inches high in the sun, up to 6 inches in the shade. Its gray-green foliage spreads rapidly by surface runners. Tiny lavender flowers spot the yellow bloom from spring through summer. They attract bees, a liability when using the plant as a lawn substitute.

CULTURE. *L. canescens* grows well in most soils in sun or part shade, but better in sun. It withstands extreme heat and sun and is very drought-resistant. Propagate by division, planting small pieces of sod 4 inches apart for fast cover.

USES. If the flowers are mowed off, a flat, tough, green mat is left that is very suitable for use as a lawn substitute in an informal setting. It is also effective around small garden pools where it can creep among rocks and up little slopes. (See page 59).

Liriope
Lilyturf

Liriope is characterized by clumps of coarse, mostly dark green, grasslike leaves up to 24 inches long and ¼ to ¾ inch wide. Like ophiopogon, with which it is sometimes confused, it is a member of the lily family. One difference between the two is that liriope is hardier. 'Big Blue' lily-turf *(L. muscari)* gets its name from its 4- to 8-inch-long, spikelike clusters of flowers that are, in fact, more violet than blue. They appear in good number among the leaves from about July into September and are followed by a few blue-black berries. This is the tallest of the lily-turfs, growing rather slowly to a height of 2 feet. It is sometimes listed as *Ophiopogon jaburan.*

Lysimachia nummularia

Lonicera japonica

Mahonia repens

Creeping lilyturf (L. spicata) is smaller in all aspects, forms a dense cover that spreads by underground stems, has pale lavender flowers, and grows at a moderate rate up to a foot high.

CULTURE. These plants have no special soil or light requirements, but are probably grown more often in partial shade, if only for reasons of landscape design. They need only light summer watering. Both are easily propagated by division. In extremely cold weather the leaves of both plants turn yellow and should be clipped off before new growth starts in spring. L. spicata is the hardiest, tolerating temperatures to −20°. L. muscari is damaged by temperatures below zero.

USES. Excellent as borders along paths, under trees, in rock gardens, or just as fill-in ground cover in small areas.

Lobularia
Sweet alyssum

Sweet alyssum (L. maritima) is a common late fall (in mild climates) or early spring bedding plant not usually considered a ground cover. It is commonly used with a new ground cover planting to cover and protect the bare soil while the planting is being established. It's very low growing (rarely more than a foot) and has narrow gray-green leaves. Quarter-size flowers appear in clusters all season long. Colors vary between dark purple and white. Some of the best varieties are 'Carpet of Snow,' white flowers, 4 inches tall; 'Tiny Tim,' white and 2 or 3 inches tall; and 'Oriental Night,' dark purple and 4 inches tall.

CULTURE. In mild areas, treat sweet alyssum as a short-lived perennial and spread seed or set out small plants as needed. In cold climates, plant in early spring for summer bloom. Full sun (some shade is okay), average soil, and normal watering is all that is necessary for them to thrive.

USES. Sweet alyssum has many garden uses: a low border, between steps (see photo, page 4), and in containers. As mentioned before, it is a perfect plant to use among slower-growing ground cover plants that haven't yet formed a tight, weed-free mat.

Lonicera
Honeysuckle

Of the many species of honeysuckle, most are vines, a few are shrubs, and one, Hall's honeysuckle (L. japonica 'Halliana'), though essentially a vine, is used as a ground cover. Evergreen in mild climates, semievergreen or deciduous in colder climates, it has the typical twining, climbing (if allowed) honeysuckle growth habit, soft, downy green leaves, and fragrant, trumpet-shaped white flowers that bloom in summer and turn a colorful yellow with age. It is exceptionally fast growing, spreading rapidly by stems that root as they cover the ground. Because of its invasive nature, it has become a pest in some parts of the country. In a flat area it can be expected to mound up to 6 feet. Other cultivars are 'Aureo-reticulata,' called the yellownet honeysuckle because of its yellow-veined leaves, a less vigorous grower, and 'Purpurea' which has purple-tinged leaves and flowers that are purple outside and white inside.

CULTURE. These honeysuckles will grow in most soils in sun or light shade, and are drought resistant. Easily propagated by division or cuttings. Honeysuckle becomes very woody and scraggly if not cut back. Hardy to −20°.

USES. For any informal, medium-to-large area where it cannot strangle shrubs or climb trees.

Nadina domestica nana

Nepeta mussini

Lysimachia
Moneywort, creeping Jenny

Moneywort *(L. nummularia)* belongs with those rapidly spreading creepers that are weeds where you don't want them (as in a lawn) and ground covers where you do. This one has small, bright green, rounded leaves on delicate rooting stems. The leaves, set oppositely, grow in sufficient number to form a wavy carpet a few inches high. Bright yellow flowers about ¾ inch in diameter bloom through the summer.

CULTURE. Moneywort will grow almost anyplace, in sun or shade, provided the soil is moist to wet. Propagate by division, starting new plants at any time.

USES. Grow it in moist, shady places where other plants, such as grass, won't grow. In fact, it is sometimes used as an aquarium plant. A natural place would be around small pools with rock sites for the foliage to creep over. Moneywort tolerates light traffic.

Mahonia   HAT S'79
Creeping mahonia

Creeping mahonia *(M. repens)* retains many of the characteristics the larger mahonia species (specifically Oregon grape, *M. aquifolium)* that make them especially interesting landscape subjects. It has striking bluish-green, spiny, holly-like leaves and 1- to 3-inch clusters of bright yellow flowers in spring. After the flowers fall, dark purple, grapelike berries form. The plant grows 1 to 2 feet high, and spreads rapidly by underground stems.

CULTURE. Creeping mahonia can be planted in full sun, but grows equally well, and looks better, in filtered shade. It deserves a good, somewhat moist soil. It can be propagated by division or from root cuttings (set out the rooted plants in spring about 10 inches apart).

USES. This is a plant for small areas such as borders, patio settings with rocks and overhead lattice — wherever it is in easy view.

Mazus
Mazus

Mazus reptans is a perennial herb that forms a thick, low mat only an inch or two high. It spreads rapidly, rooting along its stems, and sends up small, purplish-blue flowers spotted yellow and white from late spring into summer. It is evergreen in warm-winter areas; elsewhere it freezes to the ground in winter but recovers quickly in the spring.

CULTURE. This alpine plant grows best in a good, moist soil in sun or shade. Propagate by division.

USES. Particularly attractive for small-scale planting in beds, around walks, as edging. Takes light traffic.

Mentha
Corsican mint

M. requienii (Corsican mint) is the lowest growing of the many species and dozens of cultivars of mint. It spreads rapidly by underground stems, forming a soft, green carpet 1 to 3 inches high. Tiny, oval leaves, about ⅛ inch across, grow opposite

Mahonia repens

Nadina domestica nana

on slender stems and give off a strong minty fragrance when bruised. Tiny lavender-colored flowers appear in midsummer.

CULTURE. Grows equally well in sun or light shade. In a well-drained, fairly rich soil kept on the moist side, it is a vigorous grower. Easily propagated by division; set new plants 6 inches apart. Self sows. Exposed to freezing temperature for any period of time, this creeping mint will seem to disappear but usually returns in the spring. Hardy to zero°.

USES. This is a delightful ground cover for small patches anywhere in the garden, especially between stepping stones. Step on it and the delightfully fresh peppermint odor is released. In Corsica, where this plant is native, the fragrance fills the air.

Nandina
Heavenly bamboo

Heavenly bamboo (*N. domestica nana*) is a well known landscape shrub that gardeners have favored for many years. A new variety, 'Harbor Dwarf,' introduced by Georgia's Calloway Gardens, is very low (12 to 18 inches high), dense, and spreading. It is semideciduous as hardiness limits are reached (zero°) and evergreen in mild climates. Outstanding orange to bronzy-red fall color and soft, green-tinted pink in spring.

CULTURE. Nandinas tolerate some shade but foliage colors more dramatically when grown in full sun. Rich, well-drained soil is best with plenty of water through the summer. May become chlorotic in alkaline soil.

USES. The lacy, bamboolike foliage and spreading habit combine to make 'Harbour Dwarf' a very unusual, medium height ground cover. Use it near to the house or where it can be appreciated up close. It's also a good low hedge and container plant.

Nepeta
Catmint

Persian catmint (*N. mussinii*) has a year-round foliage of small, sturdy, gray-green leaves that make this herb attractive ground cover, enhanced in early summer by a lush production

Pachysandra— Spurge

For a shady spot, few ground covers work as well as pachysandra. It grows dense, creating a smooth even carpet of green. Its appearance is formal and orderly. Here are a few photographs of pachysandra at work.

Pachysandra procumbens

Newly planted bed of P. terminalis

Pachysandra terminalis

of lavender flower spikes on stems 1 to 2 feet high.

CULTURE. Needs light, well-drained soil, full sun, and periodic watering in the summer. If dead flower spikes are removed after spring blooms, a second bloom usually occurs in the fall. Hardy to −20°.

USES. Most attractive in large patches in a rock garden, as a border or behind a low-growing cover such as rupturewort (Herniaria glabra). Cats like to roll in the Persian catmint as much as they do in the standard catnip, N. cataria.

Ophiopogon
Mondo grass

Mondo grass (O. japonicus) is the most grasslike of the lilyturfs. It is identified by dense clumps of long, ⅛-inch-wide leaves that arch over into mounds 8 to 10 inches high. The leaves are dark green and coarse in texture. Small, pale purple flowers, mostly hidden among the leaves, appear in July and August followed by pea-sized blue fruit. Mondo grass spreads by means of fleshy, subsurface stems. The growth rate is quite slow until the plant is well established. A miniature version of O. japonicus, growing about half as high, is O. j. 'Nana.' O. jaburan is similar in size and growth habit to Liriope muscari, both plants often being taken for the other. The chief observable differences are that O. jaburan has green instead of brownish stems, and white, more drooping, less tightly clustered flowers. O. 'Variegatus' is a low-growing variety with white, striated leaves.

CULTURE: These plants are adaptable to most well-drained soils. In coastal areas they will grow in full sun; elsewhere they look and grow best in part shade. Both need regular summer watering. Mondo grass needs more frequent watering if exposed to full sun in a mass planting. New plants can be started by dividing clumps. Set divisions of mondo grass 6 inches apart, O. jaburan 12 inches apart. Hardy to about zero.

USES: Mondo grass looks good as a sizable planting under the shade of a large tree. In a shaded patio setting, a few dozen plants, placed about

Pachysandra as a lawn substitute.

Pachysandra terminalis

Pachysandra and phlox.

Pachysandra terminalis

8 inches apart with baby's tears *(Soleirolia soleirolii)* in between, produce a lovely, cool effect. Also makes a handsome border along paths and is useful in defining and separating a lawn and flower bed.

O. jaburan is most effective where its attractive flowers (good for cutting) and violet-blue fruits can be seen close up, as in entryways, near fences or buildings, under trees. (See photo, page 3.)

Pachysandra
Japanese spurge

Japanese spurge *(P. terminalis)* is an evergreen perennial widely used throughout the world as a ground cover in shady locations. It's hardy to —30° and remains evergreen in the most severe winters. Veined, dark green, oval leaves, 1½ to 4 inches long and lightly toothed along their upper half, grow in clusters at the top of upright stems 6 to 8 inches high. The plant spreads rapidly by underground runners to form a dense cover of essentially uniform height. The variety 'Green Carpet' is a darker green, more flowering form.

CULTURE. Japanese spurge grows only in filtered to full shade and performs best in good, somewhat moist, acidic soil. New plants can be started by division or rooted cuttings set out 6 to 12 inches apart in spring.

USES. This is the perfect ground cover to use as a large-scale planting under trees or, on a small scale, in the shade of evergreen shrubs.

Parthenocissus
Virginia creeper, woodbine

P. quinquefolia is a rambling, deciduous vine native to eastern North America. It is common to woodlands and is especially visible in the fall when it turns bright red. Boston ivy *(P. tricuspidata)* is a close relative.

Leaves are divided into leaflets. They are each attached at the same point and are 2 to 6 inches long depending on the variety. They are heavily veined and have toothed edges. The selection *P. q.* 'Engelmannii' has smaller leaflets. Inconspicuous flowers are followed by attractive blue fruits that are loved by birds. Virginia creeper hangs on with disc-tipped tendrils as it climbs. Hardy to —35°.

CULTURE. Virginia creeper is fast and easy to grow — plant it and stand back. Spaced widely, it will cover a large area cheaply and remarkably fast, though not very densely. Planted close (3 to 5 feet apart) in rich, moist soil, it can make a solid cover in one season. Takes some shade. Propagates easily by layers that form naturally or with your help (see propagation, page 89). It can also be grown from spring-sown seed.

USES. Virginia creeper readily climbs trellises and drapes over walls, attaching itself to objects by means of adhesive discs. Be careful — don't plant where it can climb (and maybe smother) shrubs or trees. Its best use is covering large, barren, rocky areas where little else grows, or as an excellent slope cover. It is also well suited to naturalistic areas where its growth doesn't need to be controlled.

Paxistima
Canby, pachistima

This is a 1-foot-high, low-maintenance ground cover *(P. canbyi)* that has been known but little used for many years. It's native to the mountains of Virginia and the Carolinas. Similar to boxwood, it has narrow ¼-inch-wide and ¼- to 1-inch-long evergreen leaves. In cold-winter areas they color slightly. This ground cover becomes dense and is long lived.

P. myrsinites or Oregon boxwood is native to the West Coast. Its leaves are slightly larger and it can become twice as tall but is easily kept low

Phlox subulata

Phlox subulata

Pernettya

Pittosporum tobiria

Lippia canescens (Phyla nodiflora)

Pittosporum tobira 'Variegata'

Polygonum cuspidatum 'Spectabilis'

Polygonum cuspidatum

Pittosporum tobira 'Wheeleri'

with pruning. Cool, moist areas in full sun are ideal but it can be grown inland with some shade and lots of water. Both species are hardy to −10°.

CULTURE. Canby paxistima grows well in either full sun or partial shade although it usually becomes more dense in full sun. It's native to rocky soil but any well-drained, slightly acidic garden soil is satisfactory. Branches root as they spread. Propagate by division or cuttings.

USES. Grows well under trees or as a low, walkway hedge. Fine for naturalistic and rock gardens.

Pernettya

P. mucronata is a handsome dwarf evergreen shrub much admired for its white to dark purple, ½-inch-wide berries that appear in great number from autumn through winter. The berries are preceded by a fine display of tiny, white, bell-shaped flowers. Berries and flowers are set off by small, shiny, dark green leaves that turn bronze in winter. The shrub spreads by underground runners, forming wide clumps up to about a foot-and-a-half high.

CULTURE. Except in hot areas, the plant is best grown in full sun; in shade, it tends to become rank and invasive. It needs an acid soil and generally cool, moist conditions. It is a good idea to group several of the color varieties together to insure cross-pollination and a good production of fruit. Propagate by division or cuttings. Hardy to −5°.

USES. Effective as a border near an entryway or along a path; also attractive as a hedge adjoining a garden pool.

Phalaris
Ribbon grass

Ribbon grass (*P. arundinacea 'picta'*) has long been used decoratively. It's hardy everywhere and is tolerant of poor growing conditions. Height is typically 3 feet; leaves are 6 to 12 inches long with a white strip. Top growth browns in fall but remains erect. Unfortunately, ribbon grass spreads by underground runners and is very invasive.

CULTURE. Easy to grow, ribbon grass is most vigorous in rich, well-drained soil but leaf variegation may disappear. In dry, heavy, or wet soil, growth slows and the plant is more manageable. In the garden, plant in containers such as a section of concrete or clay drain pipe 2½ feet long (width depending on size of clump desired). That will block the runners and prevent a takeover of your yard. Once established, it is difficult to eradicate unless contained.

USES. Beginning in spring, and through midsummer, the foliage is striking. In a perennial border or as a background to brightly colored flowers it is very handsome.

Phlox
Moss phlox

Moss phlox, *(P. subulata),* one of the standard rock garden plants, is a mat-forming perennial that produces a 4- to 6-inch-high carpet of brilliant color lasting about one month from late spring into midsummer. The ½-inch flowers, ranging in color from white to various shades of pink and red, cover the needle-like foliage completely. Individual plants grow in clumps, spreading rapidly by means of trailing stems. A number of different colored varieties, consistently named, are generally available including: 'White Delight,' 'Red Wings,' and 'Emerald Blue.' Three of the best that are consistently named are: 'White Delight,' 'Red Wings,' and 'Emerald Blue.'

CULTURE. Moss phlox is hardy, sturdy, and will grow in most soils with good drainage but needs full sun. Because seeds are not reliable in reproducing to type, propagation is best by division. Set out new plants in sping 12 to 18 inches apart. To

stimulate growth and keep a plant compact, it should be mowed about halfway to the ground after flowering. Hardy to —40°.

USES. Besides its familiar use in rock gardens, moss phlox makes an attractive small-scale border or accent plant. It is also very dramatic and attractive in large scale plantings.

Pittosporum
Mock orange, Wheeler's dwarf

The species *P. tobira* is an evergreen shrub or small tree 6 to 15 feet or more high. The variety 'Wheeler's Dwarf' grows to about 2 feet and is very useful as a ground cover for certain applications. Typically, mock orange has thick, leathery leaves, roughly oval in shape and ¾ to 1½ inches long. They are dark green and densely set along the branches, most heavily at the tips. Orange-scented white flowers that become cream-colored with age appear in dense clusters at the branch tips in spring. 'Wheeler's Dwarf' has a mounding growth habit and a moderate growth rate. A variegated variety is available that grows somewhat higher and is distinguished by light green leaves etched in creamy white at the tips.

CULTURE: This is a sturdy plant that grows well in most soils in full sun or part shade. It needs regular watering throughout the year. Pruning should be kept to a minimum. Propagate by seed or cuttings. Hardy to 20°.

USES. These are popular landscape plants in mild-climate areas where they are effective as a foreground for taller plants. They also make excellent borders, particularly along stepping-stone paths.

Polygonum
Knotweed, pink clover blossom

The few species of polygonum that can be said to qualify as ornamental ground covers are mostly mat-forming, creeping perennials that spread rapidly and invasively to the point of being pests. Nonetheless, they can be useful and they do have attractive foliage and a long blooming period. One of the most widely used is pink cloverblossom (*P. capitatum*), characterized by wiry, trailing reddish stems loosely covered by inch-long elliptical, dark green to pinkish leaves and small pink flower heads that bloom most of the year. Seen in a fairly large area, the overall effect is a dull wine-red, tangled ground cover mounding 5 to 8 inches high. *P. vaccinifolium* is a taller (to 9 inches), vigorous, less weedy-looking plant, mainly because of its rosy, upright, 3- to 4-inch-long flower spikes.

Japanese knotweed (*P. cuspidatum 'compactum')* is the hardiest of this group, easily surviving harsh winters in exposed locations. It grows 15 to 18 inches tall and blooms with pink flowers in late summer. Because it is fast growing and tolerant of poor soil, it can be terribly invasive. Use it only where it has plenty of room to spread or where its toughness is needed.

CULTURE. These plants grow best in full sun in any soil that has good drainage. Occasional watering in dry-summer areas is their only maintenance requirement. *P. capitatum* is tender to frost but comes back if the freeze is not too severe. *P. vaccinifolium* is hardier. Both are easily propagated by division or cuttings.

Potentilla verna

Potentilla verna

USES. Basically, these plants are suitable for any informal setting so long as they are contained. *P. capitatum* has been effectively used in Southern California as a parking strip planting. *P. vaccinifolium* makes a good cover on moderate slopes and can be quite striking in a rock garden.

Polystichum
Shield fern

Polystichum species are a large group of ferns, including many natives of North American forests. They are hardy and usually evergreen with sword-shaped fronds. Similar to wood ferns (dryopteris) but the rough, saw-toothed edges of the shield fern fronds are a usual, distinguishing characteristic.

The Christmas fern *(P. acrostichoides)* is native from Nova Scotia to Florida. The common name is due to the commercial availability of its fronds for Christmas decorations.

The western sword fern *(P. munitum)* is native to a range extending from Alaska, south to California, and east to Montana. Its fronds are leathery, 2 to 3½ feet long, and sometimes 10 inches wide at the base.

CULTURE. Moisture, full shade, and a humus-rich soil are the most important needs of these ferns. Propagate by dividing the underground runners in spring.

USES. Shady woodlands and rock gardens are the most common places to use these plants.

Potentilla
Cinquefoil

The cinquefoils are perennial, mostly evergreen, herbaceous plants that make highly serviceable, ornamental ground covers. They have in common five wedge-shaped, bright green coarsely toothed leaflets, small, roselike flowers, and a rapid growth rate, spreading by surface runners.

Pyracantha

Pyracantha *berries*

Rosa *'Max Graf'*

Polyantha *rose*

Rosmarinus officinalis *'Prostratus'*

Spring cinquefoil (*Potentilla verna*) is the lowest growing, forming a dense, matlike cover 3 to 6 inches high. Bright yellow, 4-petaled flowers, about ⅜ inch across, appear singly but in great number from spring well into summer.

'Willmottiae' (*Potentilla nepalensis*) grows to 10 inches high, has correspondingly larger leaflets, and flowers that are a striking deep red.

Alpine cinquefoil (*Potentilla cinerea*), popular in the Pacific Northwest, has pale yellow flowers and grows in tufts up to 4 inches high.

CULTURE. These plants grow in full sun in all but desert areas and also do well in shade. They need well-drained soil and regular watering. Propagate by division.

P. cinerea and *P. n.* 'Willmottiae' are the hardiest (to −40°). *P. verna* is somewhat less hardy (to −10°).

USES. They are excellent for medium-scale planting on slopes, under high-branched trees, or among groups of rocks where the yellow-flowering species give a cheerful feeling, the red-flowering species more drama.

Sagina subulata 'Aurea' (Scotch moss)

Sagina subulata (Irish moss)

Santolina chamaecyparissus 'Nana'

Pyracantha
Firethorn

The genera *Pyracantha* and *Cotoneaster* are composed of botanically similar evergreen shrubs sometimes difficult to distinguish at first glance. The easiest identifiable difference is that most pyracanthas have thorns, whereas most cotoneasters do not. Also, ground cover forms of cotoneaster generally have a more branching, flatter growth habit than similar forms of pyracantha. Beyond this, pyracanthas such as *P. koidzumii* 'Santa Cruz Prostrata' and the hybrid *P.* 'Ruby Mound' have denser foliage.

P. koidzumii 'Santa Cruz Prostrata' has glossy, dark green, oval leaves 1½ to 2½ inches long and serrated at the tips. In the fall, clusters of bright red berrylike fruits, attractively framed against the leaves, are formed along the ends of the branches. The fruits remain on the branches for several months. Masses of short-lived, tiny white flowers appear in the spring. The plant has a prostrate, rapidly spreading growth habit, mounding 2 to 4 feet in height. 'Ruby Mound' is notable for its long, graceful, intertwining branches. In five years a single plant will mound to 2½ feet and spread to 10 feet.

CULTURE. These plants will grow in most soils, doing best in sunny locations. Although regular watering is needed, fruit production is stimulated by keeping the soil on the dry side. Aside from the occasional prun-

ing of upward growing branches, little maintenance is required. Pyracanthas are subject to attacks of fire blight, a bacterial disease that causes the foliage and stems to turn black as if burned (see Cotoneaster for control methods).

They can be propagated by seed, or more quickly, from cuttings rooted in a light potting mix, setting out rooted plants in the spring about 18 inches apart. Hardy to 10°.

USES. These decorative plants are excellent as borders, rough hedges, or trailing down rocky slopes. The ripe fruits are edible and can be used to make a bland jelly.

Rosa
Rose

There are many roses that can be used as ground covers. Low-growing polyanthas and floribundas can be planted in mass and easily kept to a 3-foot height by occasionally pruning the upright stems.

Almost any strong-growing climbing rose can be pegged down and used as a ground cover. Tie the long canes at the tips to short stakes. Flower-bearing growth is then forced along the entire length of the cane.

'Max Graf' rose is thought to be a hybrid of *R. wichuraiana* and *R. rugosa*. At one time, it was a very popular ground cover. It grows 3- to 4-feet high and is trailing but somewhat more bushy than *R. wichuraiana*. Through the summer 3-inch pink flowers with golden centers are produced. It's hardy to −10°.

R. rugosa is called sea tomato in Japan. A tough rose, it's one of the best seashore plants withstanding considerable salt spray without damage and is hardy to −40° Leaves are glossy, and leathery, turning orange in fall. Flowers may be single or double and up to 3½ inches in diameter (many colors are available). The tomato-shaped fruits (rose hips) are brick-red, about an inch wide, and good for making preserves. The spreading, underground roots make it an excellent soil binder for slopes or sandy soil.

The Memorial rose, *R. wichuraiana*, normally grows to only 1 foot high. It's an extremely vigorous, trailing plant that can grow 10 feet in one season. It's hardy to −20° and has 2-inch white flowers in summer. Growth this fast can cause trouble, so use only in large areas where it has plenty of room to ramble.

CULTURE. Memorial rose grows best in prepared soil and full sun but tolerates poor soil. Plant 4 to 5 feet apart for a rapid cover. Propagate by cuttings or by digging the natural layers formed as the trailing stems root.

USES. This rose is unexcelled for rapidly covering large, poor soil areas. Weeds will grow through a ground cover of roses; growth is not dense enough to shade them out.

Rosmarinus
Dwarf Rosemary

A woody evergreen, well-known in its taller form for its various herbal uses. The creeping variety *Rosmarinus* *officinalis* 'Prostratus' grows slowly along the ground, spreading 4 to 8 feet. Normal height is about 8 inches, but in a mass planting can be expected to mound up to 2 feet, particularly as plants mature. It has the typically aromatic, narrow, deep green leaves, and tiny clusters of light blue ½-inch flowers that bloom the greater part of the year, most heavily in winter and spring. A form widely used in Southern California is 'Lockwood de Forest,' developed by a landscape architect after whom it is named. It is similar to 'Prostratus,' but has some erect branches that grow to 2 feet and foliage somewhat lighter in color.

CULTURE. Grows well in almost any soil so long as it has good drainage; it will not tolerate soggy soil. Rosemary is drought tolerant, but grows best with some additional water in very dry areas. Little or no fertilizer is needed. Propagate by seed, or by cuttings, setting new plants 2 feet apart. Plants get woody as they get older; control and rejuvenate by cutting out dead wood. Hardy to 10°.

USES. Excellent as a border, as a hedge, or cascading over a low wall, or grown on a slope to prevent erosion.

As an herb, use rosemary on steak, crushed into spaghetti sauce, and even with omelettes (crush and heat with the butter). In sachets, it gives a fresh and clean smell to linen drawers or closets.

Sagina
Irish moss, Scotch moss

Irish moss (*S. subulata*) and Scotch moss (*S. subulata* 'Aurea') are evergreen, perennial herbs that are alike except for color. (Both are sometimes called pearlwort.) Irish moss is deep green; Scotch moss is yellow-green. They grow in dense, rounded tufts made up of tiny, awl-shaped leaves. If allowed to, the tufts will grow together by means of creeping stems, rapidly forming a soft, mossy carpet 3 to 4 inches high. Both produce tiny white flowers in the summer.

CULTURE. These plants grow equally well in full sun or light shade. To thrive, they need a rich, well-drained soil and enough water to keep them moist but not soggy. Propagate by division. Hardy to −20°.

USES. The growth habit and interesting texture of these plants make

Santolina chamaecyparissus

Sarcococca hookeriana *'humilis'*

Sempervivum tectorum

Sempervivum tectorum

them ideal for use between stepping stones and other places where they can fill in against rocks.

Santolina
Lavender cotton

Lavender cotton (*S. chamaecyparissus*) is an evergreen shrub grown chiefly for its distinctive light gray, aromatic foliage. Close inspection reveals finely cut, woolly, green-tinged leaves densely covering the top 6 to 8 inches of woody stems that can rise as high as 30 inches. For a month or so in the summer, the foliage is partially covered by a profusion of small, round, bright yellow flower heads. This is a sturdy plant that spreads rapidly by creeping stems. A

dwarf form, 'Nana,' is available in some nurseries. *S. virens* is similar to *S. chamaecyparissus,* but has deep green, more delicate foliage, and pale yellow flowers. It grows about half as high and has a more clumpy habit.

CULTURE. Grows in any well-drained (including sandy or gravelly) soil in full sun. It is exceptionally drought resistant, requiring only occasional watering in the summer. Dies to the ground in very cold areas but usually will recover. To keep foliage compact and to prevent woody stems from showing, it should be kept pruned once a year to a foot or less in height. Propagate from cuttings taken in spring or fall. Hardy to 5°, but might be slightly damaged.

USES. Left untouched, it can serve as an informal planting against a wood fence. Clipped, it can serve as a semi-formal low hedge or as an accent plant in a patio or other small area, in which case it will rarely flower. In Europe, sachets made from the dried foliage (very powdery — use tightly woven material) have long been used as a moth repellent.

Sarcococca
Small Himalayan sarcococca

S. hookeriana 'humilis' is an attractive broadleaved evergreen shrub note-worthy for its adaptability to dense shade. It stays low, rarely over 2 feet, and spreads several feet by under-

Sedum

With hundreds of varieties to choose from, there's a sedum for every garden. Here are a few.

Sedum acre

Sedum acre *with* liriope *in foreground*

Sedum guatemalense (x rubrotinctum)

Sedum rupestre

ground runners. Its most attractive feature is glossy, dark green foliage. The leaves are 1 to 2 inches long and about ½-inch wide. Fragrant white flowers in spring are followed by black berries. Hardy to −20°.

CULTURE. The most important cultural factors are acidic soil generously amended with organic matter and shade. Direct sunlight or reflected heat are damaging as is too much wind. Water frequently until established, then water normally. Pinch stem tips to promote horizontal spreading and dense growth. Propagate by division of the creeping roots, cuttings, or seed. Check for scale insects (see page 91).

USES. Excellent massed in heavily shaded areas where little else grows or as a low border in front of tall-growing shrubs such as rhododendron and camellia.

Sedum
Stonecrop

There are over 300 species and at least twice as many varieties of sedum. There are tiny sedums forming mats only an inch or two high and others that reach to two feet. A few flower abundantly; others are shy bloomers. The beauty of the plants is in the shape and color of their leaves. They are, by definition, rock plants, although their use is by no means confined to rock gardens. There are species that are effective on slopes, between stepping stones, as a mass planting, as container plants, and especially, blended with other ground covers such as the prostrate junipers. Sedums root easily from cuttings; they even propagate themselves from broken leaves. Sedums are not particular about soil or water. As a guide, use the least amount of water that will keep them healthy and colorful.

Sedum acre, called mossy or gold-moss stonecrop, has tiny leaves less than ¼-inch long. It is vigorous and grows to a height of only 2 inches. It is perfectly happy growing between stepping stones and in rock crevices. Stays green through the coldest winters; hardy to −35°.

Sedum spectabilis

Sedum confusum

Sedum telephium

Sedum album is a fast-growing creeping evergreen that forms a green mat 3 to 6 inches high. In the summer it sends up 8-inch stems covered at the top by delicate branching clusters of tiny, star-shaped white flowers that attract bees. There are a number of varieties, some with purple foliage and yellow-green or pinkish flowers. Hardy to −20°.

Sedum anglicum is a popular, hardy, evergreen creeper that forms a dense, mosslike, dark green mat about 3 inches high. Sends up 3- to 5-inch stems in the summer covered by lightly branched stems bearing pinkish white flowers. Hardy to −20°.

Sedum brevifolium, an evergreen creeper, forms a bright green mat 2 inches high. It has wiry, somewhat woody stems and, in summer, white flowers streaked with pink. Good rock garden plant. Hardy to −20°.

Sedum confusum is a relatively tender sedum. It is an evergreen, somewhat shrubby, branching plant to about one foot high. The leaves are light green, the summer flowers are yellow. A good ground cover for level ground or slopes. A desirable plant that fills in quickly. Hardy to 10°.

Sedum dasyphyllum, a handsome evergreen (annual in very cold climates) that forms a low-tufted (1 to 2 inches) bluish-green mat lightly covered by white flowers in summer and fall. Needs full sun. Hardy to 0°.

Sedum guatemalense (x rubrotinctum), commonly known as pork and beans or whisky nose, is deservedly popular. Stems are 3 to 6 inches in length, the top half covered with clusters of beanlike green leaves that become bronzy red with exposure to full sun. Excellent in every way sedums are used. Seeds itself so easily that it can crowd out smaller species. Produces yellow flowers in the spring, but it's the evergreen foliage that counts. Hardy to 10°.

Sedum morganianum. This is the popular donkey's- or burro's-tail, so named because of a growth habit which produces long (6 inches to 3 feet) trailing stems densely covered with short, fleshy, gray-green leaves. It is really not suitable as a standard ground cover, but in mild areas (not reliably hardy below freezing) can be very effective on a slope, draped over walls, or as a house plant. In contrast to most sedums, it requires good soil, some shade, and regular watering in the summer.

Sedum oaxacanum is a spreading, evergreen plant having 6-inch long brownish stems, covered mostly at the ends with rosettes of thick, grayish-green leaves. Yellow flowers in the spring. Tolerates temperatures to 10°.

Sedum palmeri (compressum), an attractive, flowering evergreen, has fleshy gray-green leaves in loose rosettes at the top of stems 6 to 8 inches high. Beautiful yellow flowers bloom from April to summer.

Sedum sarmentosum is a hardy, spreading evergreen with yellow-green leaves; grows about 6 inches high. Has relatively large, bright yellow flowers that appear in profusion in the spring, covering the foliage. Hardy to −40°.

Sedum spurium is a creeping, nearly evergreen perennial with rounded green leaves in loose rosettes forming a 3- to 6-inch mat. Sometimes called 'Dragon's Blood,' this sedum is very popular in colder sections of the country. Clusters of light red, starry flowers blooming in late summer. Hardy to −40°.

Sempervivum
Hen-and-chickens

Hen-and-chickens *(S. tectorum)* are plants well-known to American gardeners, having arrived with the earliest settlers. They are very easily grown, requiring only sun and good drainage. Leaves are fleshy and grow in rosettes. There are many different selections and varieties possessing different colors and heights. All are hardy to −20°.

CULTURE. Watering is not usually necessary except during unusually long droughts. In a good soil, growth will be faster. Propagate by separating offsets.

USES. Planted around rocks, they will quickly fill in cracks and crevices. On dry slopes they can outgrow most weeds. In medieval years, these were used for binding soil on the sod roofs of cottages. The species name *tectorum* is a Latin word meaning "roof."

Soleirolia
Baby's-tears

Baby's-tears *(S. soleirolii, Helxine soleirolii)* is a creeping, mosslike plant that forms a dense, soft carpet 1 to 3 inches high. The foliage is composed of tiny, light green, rounded leaves growing in a tight mat.

CULTURE. This is a plant for shade, rich soil, and moisture. It is quickly killed by direct sun, drought, or subfreezing temperature. Propagate by division, planting sections 6 to 12 inches apart. For outdoor use only in warmest regions.

USES. Provides a cool, delicate effect planted at the base of trees or shade plants like ferns, camellias and azaleas. The plant is well named for it is

Teucrium chamaedrys

Stachys byzantina

Vancouveria hexandra

as fragile as a baby's tear. A few steps will not kill it, but the footprint will remain for days.

Stachys
Lamb's-ears

The herb, lamb's-ears *(S. byzantina)* got its name from its shape and woolly softness. It's hardy to —20° and grows to 18 inches high in clumps 3 feet wide. Leaves are 4 inches long and a silvery gray color that contrasts well with green plants. Purple flowers come in summer on 1-foot spikes.

CULTURE. This is an easily grown plant needing only good drainage and full sun. Cold winters may damage some leaves so plants are usually cut back in the spring. Clumps can be divided at any time of year.

USES. The gray leaves stand out dramatically against greens such as wild strawberry. They also combine with other gray-foliaged plants such as blue fescue, dianthus, woolly thyme, and snow-in-summer.

Teucrium
Germander

T. chamaedrys is an undramatic but neat, tough little plant. Stems 6 to 8 inches in height are closely covered over their full length by small, serrated, medium green leaves to form a thick cover. Tiny, rosy-lavender blossoms appear on the upper parts in the summer. Growth rate is rapid by spreading underground root stems.

CULTURE. Grows in any well-drained soil, best in full sun but also in light shade. This is a drought-tolerant, heat-loving plant requiring only occasional summer watering. Easily propagated by division or cuttings. Set plants 12 to 15 inches apart.

USES. Left untouched, effective in large, informal areas; also in desert and rock gardens where its deep roots serve as a binder in sandy soil. Takes well to shearing — it often serves as an excellent low formal hedge or walk border.

Thymus
Thyme, mother-of-thyme

Listed here are varieties of the herb thyme most commonly used as ground covers. There is some confusion with names of *thymus*. Home gardeners should be alert to the possibility of finding them under different names at his local nursery.

These plants are characteristically prostrate or creeping, have tiny, opposite leaves sometimes covered with delicate white hairs and very small flowers on upright spikes. They are, above all, aromatic, releasing that delightful fragrance familiar in cooking, when they are rubbed or walked on. Culturally, they present few problems. They grow in almost any well-drained soil, prefer full sun but will take some shade, and need regular watering in hot summer areas. Beyond periodic trimming to keep them tidy,

Vaccinium

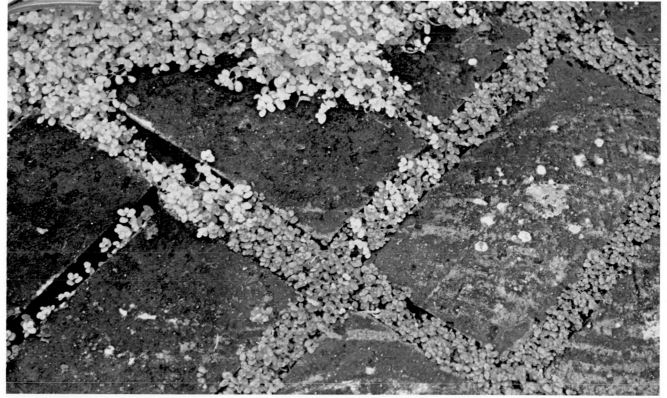
Soleirolia soleirolii

they need no other care. They are easily propagated by division or cuttings taken in the spring. Set new plants 6 to 12 inches apart. All are very hardy to −30° or −40°.

Creeping thyme, or mother-of-thyme, *(T. serpyllum),* forms a flat green mat. Upright stems, 3 to 6 inches high, are loosely covered with whorls of tiny, pale lavender flowers that bloom from late spring through summer. Excellent as a border or in a rock garden; also good on dry slopes. Light traffic.

White creeping thyme *(T.s. 'Albus')* forms a denser lower mat covered in spring and summer by a profusion of tiny white flowers. Grows 2 to 4 inches high. Excellent between stepping stones. Thymus tolerates light traffic.

Pink creeping thyme *(T.s. 'Roseus'),* same as 'Albus' but with pink flowers.

Lemon thyme *(T. citriodorus)* is similar to *T. serpyllum* but with lemon-scented foliage.

Woolly thyme *(T. pseudolanuginosus* or *T. lanuginosus)* has tiny, gray-green, soft woolly leaves that form a dense carpet 2 to 3 inches high. Its somewhat mounding growth habit makes it strikingly effective between stepping stones, spilling over a boulder or a low bank, or simply alone as a small accent plant. It has tiny pink flowers which seldom appear.

Common thyme *(T. vulgaris)* is coarser and taller (6 to 10 inches) flowers.

than *T. serpyllum* and is better used as a low hedge. Cultivars 'Argenteus,' 'Fragrantissimus,' and 'Roseus' may be available at some nurseries.

A member of our staff says this about thyme: "Creeping thyme gives off a warm, indolent fragrance in hot weather. It attracts bees with ease, and a really choice honey can be made with its nectar. Use dried thyme in stews, crush on lamb chops, or sprinkle on broiled salmon. Add thyme to any food you'd serve with white wine."

Tiarella
Foamflower

T. cordifolia is an attractive, deciduous perennial that makes an excellent

Vinca minor — Periwinkle

Vinca minor is one of the best evergreen ground covers. Excellent for a naturalistic setting, as a slope cover, or trailing over a wall. An easy-to-grow plant.

Vinca minor *'Silver Queen'*

Vinca minor

Vinca minor

ground cover in moist, shaded areas. It is native to woodlands of eastern Canada and the United States and is a close relative of coralbells (heuchera). The plant's most outstanding feature is the beautiful, fluffy clusters of white flowers that cover the plant in May. The lobed leaves (somewhat like a maple leaf) are 2 to 4 inches in diameter. They often offer brilliant color in the fall. Flowers are on 12-inch stalks. Although white is the most common color, there are selections of pinkish, purple, and other shades of red. Spreads vigorously by underground runners and is hardy to −30°.

CULTURE. Native to forests and woodlands, this plant prefers a moist,

humus-rich, slightly acidic soil. It's best if clumps are divided every two or three years. Propagate by root divisions in spring or fall.

USES. This is a fairly tolerant woodland plant that makes a fine ground cover in naturalistic gardens, shaded rock gardens, and in small shaded niches around the home.

Vaccinium
Mountain cranberry, lingonberry

Mountain cranberry *(V. vitis-idaea 'minus')* is native to northern United States and Canada, its range extending from Alaska to Massachusetts. A blueberry relative, it needs moist, acidic soil to grow. Leaves are about ½ inch long, evergreen and glossy.

Flowers are white to red, bell-shaped, and about ¼ inch long. Mountain cranberry spreads by underground runners and makes a dense, even mat 8 inches or less in height. Red berries are useful for preserves and syrups. Reliably hardy to −10°.

CULTURE. In mountainous coolsummer regions, full sun is accepted if plants are generously watered. Otherwise grow in partial shade. Propagate by dividing the creeping roots or by transplanting sodlike clumps.

USES. Mountain cranberry is most useful in naturalistic gardens where it can make a floor for shrubs such as large-growing rhododendrons. A single plant in a garden will spread to form a small mat.

Vinca minor 'Aureo-variegata'

Vinca minor

Vinca minor

Veronica spicata

Vinca major

Viola priceana

Vancouveria
American barrenwort

This is a Pacific Northwest native that is closely related to the epimediums (page 28). American barrenwort (*V. hexandra*) grows to 1 or 1½ feet tall. White flowers (½ inch) appear in May through June. The leaves are delicate, light green, and they die to the ground each winter. Hardy to −10°.

CULTURE. Vancouveria grows naturally in the shade of the coast redwoods. There, the soil is acidic and high in organic matter. Temperatures are cool and there is plenty of moisture.

USES. This is an excellent ground cover plant where it is well adapted.

Waldsteinia fragarioides

Viola priceana

Combine with ferns and epimediums around the base of trees and in shaded beds. The cut foliage is becoming in bouquets.

Veronica
Speedwell

The speedwells are classic garden accent and border plants. The species listed here have been chosen for their proven practicality, their popularity, and their different growth habits. All are evergreen perennials (in most of the country) with shiny green, notched, oval to lance-shaped leaves and attractive flowers, mostly in spikes, that bloom in the summer. They are vigorous, fast growers that can take over a lawn, serving as a lawn substitute (if so desired), but will not take traffic.

Woolly speedwell (*V. incana*) forms a gray-green, tight, 6-inch mat with pale blue flowers on spikes that rise 6 inches higher.

Hungarian speedwell (*V. latifolia* 'prostrata') has a similar growth habit but spreads more widely and has dark green foliage. Hardy to 0°.

Creeping speedwell (*V. repens*), the lowest growing, forms a 4-inch dark green mat dotted in spring and early summer with clusters of small blue flowers. It makes an excellent lawn substitute; hardy to −10°.

CULTURE. These plants grow in full sun or part shade. They need good soil and regular watering throughout the year. They are easily propagated by division.

USES. These veronicas make good paving plants particularly in shady areas. They can soften the edges of steps or paved areas and be used as a bulb cover. Anyone who has fought to keep the weedy veronicas out of a lawn knows their value as lawn substitutes.

Viburnum
Dwarf highbush cranberry

V. opulus 'Nanum' is a dwarf form of the 12-foot cranberry bush; it grows no taller than 3 feet. Its leaves are lobed like a maple's and turn bright red in fall. Unlike its full-size relative, this variety rarely flowers or fruits. Its hardiness is good (to −35°).

CULTURE. Set on 1-foot centers, plants will eventually fill in and completely shade out the ground. It does best in semishade and tolerates poor and wet soils. Very little maintenance is necessary once established.

USES. The dwarf highbush cranberry is excellent for low borders or hedges. Because of slow growth, it is best used as a ground cover for small areas.

Vinca
Periwinkle, myrtle

Periwinkle (*V. minor*) is one of the best evergreen ground covers. It has been used in American gardens for over 200 years and thrives in many varied climates. Periwinkle is very flat growing, usually only reaching 6 inches high. Leaves are dark green and about 1 inch long. Flowers have 5 petals, are 1 inch in diameter and usually a lilac-blue color. The best varieties are 'Alba,' white flowers; 'Atropurpurea,' purple flowers; 'Aureo-variegata,' leaves spotted with yellow; and larger, deeper blue flowers. ('Bowlesii' is the only variety that is more clump-forming than trailing.) Hardy to −30°.

Myrtle (*V. major*) is very similar, but is more coarse, grows three to four times as high, and is less hardy—to −10°. Two color variants having mottled white or gold leaves are available.

CULTURE. Vincas grow best in partial shade and well-prepared soil. Near the coast or in cool areas, they grow in full sun. Water frequently during extended droughts and fertilize periodically to sustain vigorous growth. Propagate by division or from stem or root cuttings. Fungus disease can cause problems but is controllable with fungicides that contain Benlate. Spray early in spring as new growth emerges. Two monthly follow-up sprays may be necessary.

USES. *V. minor* has good color, form, and a texture that makes it compatible with many landscapes. It is an excellent choice for medium-scale plantings, particularly in the filtered shade of large trees. *V. major* is useful as a large-scale ground cover on a slope particularly in naturalistic gardens.

Viola
Violet

Pansies, violas, and violets are all herbaceous perennials belonging to the genus *Viola*. Pansies and violas are commonly grown as annuals or biennials; a few species of violets are useful ground covers.

Violets are 3- to 6-inch high plants with bright green leaves, and summer-blooming, ¾-inch-wide flowers in a wide range of solid and mixed colors. They grow in tufts and spread by creeping runners. The Australian violet (*V. hederacea*) forms a tight, leafy carpet heavily dotted in summer with typical violet flowers, mostly blue in the center, fading to white at the tips.

The sweet violet (*V. odorata*), the classic popular violet, has dark green leaves and mostly fragrant flowers. Numerous varieties are available with flowers of different size and color. Among them are 'Royal Robe,' large, deep blue flowers; 'Marie Louise,' fragrant double white and lavender flowers; 'Royal Elk,' long-stemmed, single, fragrant, violet-colored flowers; 'Charm,' small white flowers; and 'Rosina,' pink flowers.

The Confederate violet (*V. priceana*) is stemless, has large leaves up to 5 inches wide, and flat, pansylike, whitish flowers veined violet-blue.

CULTURE. To look their best, violets need partial shade, plenty of water, and rich, moist soil. They can be propagated by seed, or, quicker, by division. Sweet violet and Confederate violet are hardy almost everywhere. *V. hederacea* is much less hardy.

USES. These plants are for small-scale planting — as borders, in beds, or around large-leaved evergreen shrubs.

Waldsteinia
Barren strawberry

The barren strawberry (*W. fragarioides*) is for those who admire the foliage of the strawberry but do not want the fruit. It has the typical 3-leaflet evergreen leaves that are toothed at the tips, 5-petaled yellow flowers like *Duchesnea indica*, and the same creeping growth habit. It forms a thick mat 4 to 10 inches high in sun or shade. It will not take drought or extended periods of heat. Like other strawberry plants, it can be propagated by seed or division. It is hardy to −20°.

W. ternata is best adapted to southern Canada and the northern U.S. In both sunny and shaded locations, it maintains an even 4-inch height. Leaves are evergreen to semi-evergreen and glossy green in color. Leaflets are smaller than those of *W. fragarioides* — about ½- to 1¼-inch long. This is a compact-growing plant with few problems.

CULTURE. The waldsteinias are widely adapted, easy-to-grow plants, but do best when provided with ample water in a well-drained soil. Plant on 12-inch centers; propagate by either seeds or division.

USES. These are too frequently overlooked plants. They have been used on banks, in rock gardens, and around homes successfully.

Xanthoriza
Yellow-root

X. simplicissima is an easily grown deciduous shrub that deserves to be better known by home gardeners. It grows very uniformly to a 2-foot height. Toothed or lobed leaves are 1 to 3 inches long and turn a beautiful yellow-orange in the fall. Tiny purplish flowers in drooping clusters appear in May usually before the leaves unfold. Spreading roots and stems have an attractive yellow bark. Hardy to −30°.

CULTURE. Yellow-root is tolerant of many soils but grows most luxuriantly in moist soil. It prefers full sun but is not bothered by medium shade. The easiest method of propagation is to simply dig clumps but root cuttings is another method of starting new plants.

USES. This is a good plant for low, wet spots — areas for which the choice of plants is small.

Waldsteinia ternata

Viburnum opulus 'Nanum'

A short course in landscaping with ground covers

Ground covers are the most versatile, and in some situations, the most valuable of all landscape plants. In the following chapter the experts — landscape architects — offer their thoughts on ground cover landscaping.

This chapter is devised to be a short course in ground cover landscaping, so that you, the homeowner, can use these plants to the best advantage. To create such a course, we went to the experts — the landscape architects. We asked their opinions and their philosophies. So that you could see their work, we've included photographs and plans of professionally landscaped sites.

Harmony and accent

Generally, an ideal landscape could be defined as one where the viewer isn't aware of any one element. A balanced blending of separate and diverse plant materials creates an overall peaceful and tranquil mood.

This blending is one of the most important functions of ground covers. Their variety of growth habits, foliage, color, and texture, and their range of cultural requirements allow them to fit into any landscape, into any place. Ground covers blend so well into our outdoor environment, we often take their presence for granted. But without this versatile group of plants, a landscape would be starkly incomplete.

Every home landscape also needs some contrast to keep it from becoming monotonous. A visual focal point brought about by plant color, shape, or texture will keep the viewer's eyes and attention from wandering, thus creating interest in the landscape.

◁

Entry way to the Haskell garden nursery features a low hedge of Japanese barberry (Berberis thunbergii *'Crimson Pygmy'*) *and a bright green carpet of kinnikinnick* (Arctostaphylos uva-ursi). *Color of the full moon maple* (Acer japonicum *'Aureum'*) *in background perfectly matches the crimson shade of the low barberry hedge.*

Focalization can be obtained by individual ground cover plants or masses of ground cover plantings. Ground covers planted adjacent to a lawn will break up the expanse of green, adding interesting lines and textures. Splashes of ground cover color (including varying shades of green) against stone walls, between paths and steps, or alone as specimen plants will bring about this necessary diversification.

Ground covers as accent plants can be the exclamation point of your landscape statement. They may make a purely decorative point — a mound of Irish moss — or they may be the practical solution to a problem area —

ajuga grouped to cover the exposed roots at the base of a tree.

You must use any accent plant with restraint, however. Too many varieties with contrasting colors and textures will create a hodgepodge rather than the integrated landscape you set out to design.

An evergreen garden

The photos shown here and on the two following pages belong to the nursery and garden center of Allen C. Haskell, New Bedford, Mass. Mr. Haskell's garden nursery is a testimony to a frequently forgotten garden color — *green*. Too often gardeners tend to think of color only

Entwining foliage of 'Blue Rug' juniper creates a close-knit mat of evergreen ground cover.

in reds, blues, yellows, and oranges — the colors of seasonal annuals. But too many colors in a garden can create an unsettling mood. By using evergreen ground covers. Haskell demonstrates how well green works: by itself, and as the perfect backdrop for seasonal displays.

There is a tremendous variety of evergreen ground covers, Haskell today. Our juniper gallery on page 46-47 is a prime example. Most evergreens are quite hardy and, once established require only minimal care.

Evergreen ground covers can become the foundation of your garden. The seasonal colors come and go, but the evergreens stay beautiful the entire year.

Professionally speaking

The following discussion on landscaping with ground covers is written by Mr. Morgan "Bill" Evans, of Malibu, California. Evans could be called the professional's professional. — for 21 years he was Director of Landscape Design for Disneyland in California and Disneyworld in Florida; he is a past president of the American Institute of Landcape Architects. He has landscaped miniature Matterhorn mountains and has designed life-size animal topiaries. Here are his words.

"Nothing is more gracious or complimentary to the landscape than a great sweep of velvet grass. In some circumstances, nothing else should even be considered. By the same token, however, there are also many sites where grass is simply not the answer. In addition to the obvious reasons (terrain, light conditions, high maintenance) there are many more subtle design considerations where an inspired use of just the right ground covers will produce a gratifying effect.

"The great range of plants suitable for ground covering tasks affords opportunities not present with turf. Sloping or rolling ground unsuited for lawn culture can be turned to distinct aesthetic advantage by playing up the grade differentials. Or, where confronted with an uninteresting level plane, motion in three dimensions can be created by the import of fill soil or sculpturing of existing earth, again to provide the subtle contours best enhanced by appropriate cover plants. In extreme cases where man-made sites present unlovely cut-and-fill slopes, rescue is possible and their grade adjustment achieved with the help of boulders, stone riffraff, railroad ties, and the correct choice of plant material. A sensitively molded earth form can be treated with the kind of cover that exactly preserves the flowing lines; or an offensive, mechanical slope can be so artfully dis-

An evergreen garden

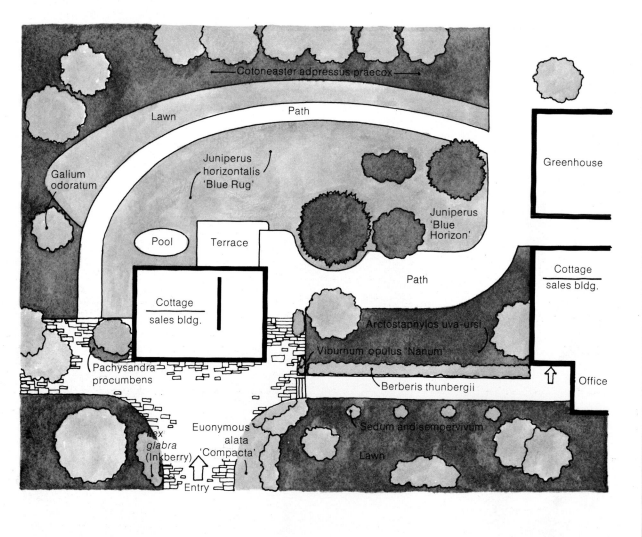

A low-growing bed of 'Blue Horizon' juniper takes the place of a lawn, but doesn't need a lot of maintenance.

Cotoneaster adpressus 'praecox' blends the lawn and trees into a unified landscape.

guised by well-chosen plantings that its shape is unseen.

"The interplay of natural stone, masonry, or wood with select ground covers opens up new dimensions literally and figuratively. Steps, paths, and terraces can be crisply or subtly delineated; pebbles and bark wood rounds are mutually complementary elements to incorporate in ground cover design solutions.

"Recently developed techniques for the reproduction of natural rock forms offer an exciting new approach in which difficult grade conditions can

be converted from a vice to a virtue. The process evolved over several years and with the input of various artisans, the most successful of whom now offer custom service. Methods vary, but in general it is now possible to produce surprisingly realistic shapes and textures simulating nearly every natural rock condition — dry, or incorporating a wide variety of water effects. The final product can be purely aesthetic or functional. It can be poured in place, as a reinforced retaining wall, for example. Crevices, ledges, and planting pockets are part

of the design and permit the culture of appropriate trailing plant materials for a harmonious marriage of the natural and the artificial.

"It is a long design stride from the above to the simple and straightforward treatment of irregular terrain with native plants. Each region has its own indigenous plant communities which invariably include spreading, sprawling, or creeping covers.

"The best of these subjects found their way into commercial culture and catalogs long ago; hybrids and type selections have multiplied the op-

Sempervivums and sedums grow outdoors in this container without protection at the Haskell garden nursery.

Juniper planting ('Blue Horizon') gives added interest to this landscape view.

Bright blue Picea pungens 'Glauca Prostrata' *is a striking accent in the landscape.*

tions, in some cases to a bewildering degree (junipers, for example). But in almost every part of this land where gardening is pursued, the opportunity to cover your particular earth with essentially low-maintenance native plants is present. In the low rainfall zones of Southern California and Arizona, we have had to borrow from the Mediterranean, West Australia, and South Africa to supplement our rather meager native supply, but these imports have so comfortably fitted into the local scene that we may be pardoned for treating them as our own.

"Scale plays an important part in plant selection. This aspect is reflected not only in specific leaf size, but habit of growth — compact vs. arching; creeping or matlike as opposed to self-supporting, horizontal habit. There are plants that blend into a continuous texture for sweeping lines and plants that are most attractive as individuals.

"No discussion of ground cover options would be complete without reference to the succulents. The term succulent is somewhat imprecise because plants so identified belong to widely divergent families, but in a broad sense, those subjects that tend to be fleshy, plump, and full of juice or sap are lumped together as succulents. They are native to an astonishing geography, from Siberia through the tropics to the tip of South America and South Africa. Although some are extremely hardy and moisture tolerant, as a class they are best adapted to warm, dry climates where their camel-like ability to store water carries them for long periods without irrigation. Of infinite form and behavior, many are distinguished by spectacular flowers as well as attractive color tones in foliage. As with ground covers in general, the choices are legion in size, scale, posture and performance. In the warmer sections of the country, an entire landscape design may be executed with succulents for impressive results.

"We have scarcely mentioned grass since the opening paragraph but of course there are many pleasing combinations of grass and ground cover. Some distinction should be made between grasses like *Festuca ovina 'glauca'* or *Zoysia tenuifolia* 'Aurel,' and conventional turfgrasses. The former is regarded as a ground cover per se, whereas turfgrass of whatever breed requires a special kind of maintenance absent in ground cover culture.

"In so many of our contemporary architectural designs, modest expanses of trim grass, freeform or

A low-maintenance landscape

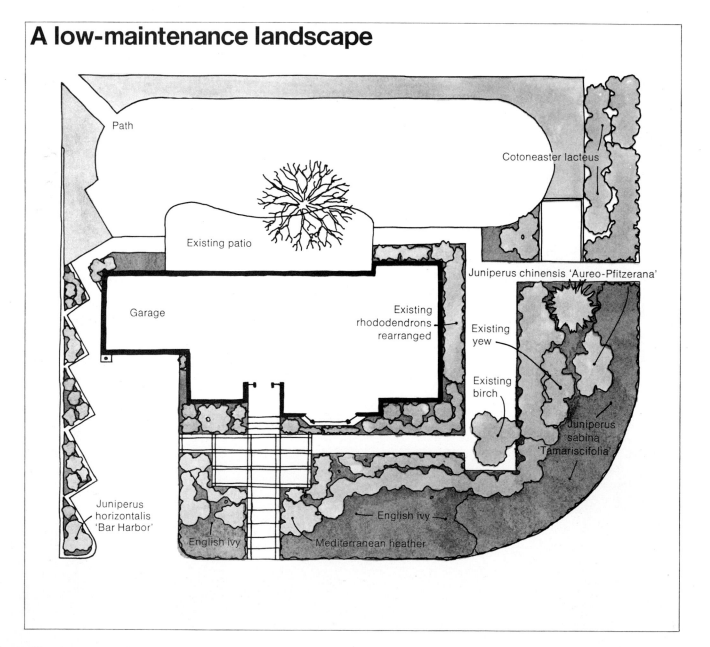

Path

Cotoneaster lacteus

Existing patio

Juniperus chinensis 'Aureo-Pfitzerana'

Garage

Existing rhododendrons rearranged

Existing yew

Existing birch

Juniperus sabina 'Tamariscifolia'

Juniperus horizontalis 'Bar Harbor'

English ivy

English ivy

Mediterranean heather

geometrical, are desirable to complement certain structural elements. Shadow patterns, including those of trees, are better revealed on lawn than ground cover, for example. Turf and ground cover associations often flatter each other.

"When a planting line is created, it is usually a good idea to keep it going as far as practicable, seeking some motion but avoiding abrupt change of direction. Tiered perspectives are attainable by the use of carefully selected species, thus adding a third dimension to a flat site.

"A word of caution — whether the job be a result of your own doing or contracted with a professional — satisfaction can be short-lived if weeds invade. One can live with certain intruders when the grass is cut weekly, and selective weed controls are a welcome assist, but nothing is more tiresome or frustrating than battling entrenched weeds among ground covers. When the earth has been shaped and graded, when the header boards are in place and soil has been suitably turned and amended, be sure that the correct herbicides are carefully applied. As an extra precaution, regular irrigation should be practiced for a reasonable period to coax

Residence entryway is designed to invite people to the front door. Mediterranean heather (Erica mediterranea) *and English ivy* (Hedera helix) *are attractive, low-maintenance plants, require only a once-a-year trimming.*

A street-side view of home demonstrates how well ivy and juniper companion together.

Front of home from another angle. Note how ivy and heather integrate at entrance.

out any fugitive weeds before the finished planting.

"Good ground cover landscaping is not easy, but with some study and much prudent thought (plus honest toil), it is within reach of most home gardeners."

A low-maintenance landscape

The photos and plan shown here and on the two preceding pages are of a professionally landscaped site in Portland, Oregon. Barbara Fealy, the landscape architect for the project, describes how she used ground covers to transform a high-maintenance landscape to one of low maintenance.

"Originally, this property was planted exclusively in lawn. This became quite a chore, because it demanded constant maintenance to look its best. It was decided that the area should be redesigned for easier care. In the process, a new entrance walk and porch were built. The lawn area was regraded to create an easy, constant slope. At the entrance of the house, Mediterranean heather was planted. The remaining area was given to English ivy, planted at 1-foot intervals. Two varieties of junipers were also used.

"For obtaining quick and lasting results, attention was given to obtain a thorough preparation of the soil. To the existing heavy clay soil, pulverized bark, and fertilizers were thoroughly mixed to provide the necessary well-drained loam. In two seasons the new planting had a completely mature look. Maintenance was reduced to once-a-year clipping of the heather and the ivy."

A close look at Mediterranean heather reveals its texture and mounding habit.

Dense mat of Juniper (J. sabina 'Tamariscifolia') protects gradual slope, and forms an attractive evergreen buffer zone between the house and the street.

Selection guide for special situations

Because of the variety of cultural requirements and growth habits available, many ground covers are naturally better adapted than others to grow in certain situations. The following lists ground covers recommended for special uses and situations found in the home landscape.

Easy to grow

Ajuga reptans .... Bugleweed
Arctostaphylos uva-ursi .... Kinnikinnick
Cotoneaster
Euonymus fortunei
  'Colorata' .... Wintercreeper
Hedera helix .... English ivy
Hypericum calycinum .... Aaron's beard
Juniperus .... Juniper
Pachysandra
  terminalis .... Japanese spurge
Potentilla verna .... Spring cinquefoil
Sedum .... Stonecrop
Vinca minor .... Dwarf periwinkle

Drought resistant

Aegopodium podagraria ......Goutweed
Arctostaphylos uva-ursi .... Kinnikinnick
Artemisia ...... Dusty-miller, wormwood
Comptonia peregrina .... Sweet fern
Coronilla varia .... Crown vetch
Cytisus .... Broom
Festuca ovina 'glauca' ...... Blue fescue
Genista .... Broom
Helianthemum nummularium .. Sun rose
Hemerocallis .... Daylily
Juniperus .... Juniper
Phalaris arundinacea 'picta' Ribbon-grass
Polygonum cuspidatum
  'compactum' .... Fleece flower
Santolina
  chamaecyparissus ... Lavender cotton
Sedum .... Stonecrop

Full sun

Arabis .... Rock cress
Achillea tomentosa ...... Woolly yarrow
Arctostaphylos uva-ursi ..... Kinnikinick
Artemisia schmidtiana ..... Angel's hair
Cerastium
  tomentosum .... Snow-in-summer
Comptonia peregrina .... Sweet fern
Cotoneaster .. Cotoneaster (low-growing)
Cytisus .... Broom
Helianthemum nummularium ... Sun rose
Juniperus .... Juniper
Phlox subulata .... Moss pink
Pyracantha koidzumii
  'Santa Cruz' .. 'Santa Cruz' pyracantha
Rosa .... Rose

Full sun continued

Santolina
  chamaecyparissus ... Lavender cotton
Sedum .... Stonecrop

Sun or partial shade

Aegopodium podagraria ......Goutweed
Ajuga .... Bugleweed
Bergenia
Campanula .... Bellflower
Epimedium .... Barrenwort
Hedera helix .... English ivy
Hypericum calycinum .... Aaron's beard
Liriope spicata .... Lilyturf
Mahonia repens ..... Creeping mahonia
Ophiopogon japonicus .... Mondo grass
Paxistima canbyi ...... Canby paxistima
Polygonum .... Knotweed

Tolerate deep shade

Adiantum pedatum ..... Five-finger fern
Asarum .... Ginger
Athyrium
  goeringianum .. Japanese painted fern
Convallaria majalis .... Lily-of-the-valley
Dryopteris .... Wood fern
Epimedium .... Barrenwort
Galium odoratum .... Sweet woodruff
Hedera helix .... English ivy
Pachysandra terminalis Japanese spurge
Sagina subulata .. Irish and Scotch moss
Sarcococca humilis .. Sweet sarcococca
Soleirolia soleirolii .... Baby's-tears
Vinca minor .... Dwarf periwinkle
Viola odorata .... Sweet violet

Lawn alternatives (large areas)

Comptonia peregrina .... Sweet fern
Coronilla varia .... Crown vetch
Dianthus deltoides .... Maiden pink
Duchesnea indica ..... Mock strawberry
Hedera ....Ivy
Hypericum calycinum .... Aaron's beard
Juniperus .... Juniper (spreading)
Lonicera .... Honeysuckle
Pachysandra terminalis Japanese spurge
Polygonum cuspidatum
  'compactum' .... Fleece flower
Potentilla .... Cinquefoil
Sedum
Vinca .... Periwinkle

Slope stabilizers

Akebia quinata .... Five-leaf akebia
Arctostaphylos uva-ursi .... Kinnikinnick
Comptonia peregrina .... Sweet fern
Cotoneaster .. Cotoneaster (low-growing)
Hedera .... Ivy
Hemerocallis .... Daylily
Hypericum calycinum .... Aaron's beard
Juniperus .... Juniper (low-growing)
Lonicera .... Honeysuckle

Slope stabilizers continued

Parthenocissus
  quinquefolia .... Virginia creeper
Phalaris arundinacea 'picta' Ribbon-grass
Polygonum cuspidatum
  'compactum' .... Fleece flower
Pyracantha koidzumii
  'Santa Cruz' .. 'Santa Cruz' pyracantha
Rosa .... Rose (low-growing)
Vinca ....Periwinkle

Drape and trail

Arctostaphylos uva-ursi .... Kinnikinnick
Artemisia ...... Dusty-miller, wormwood
Campanula .... Bellflower
Cerastium
  tomentosum .... Snow-in-summer
Cotoneaster .. Cotoneaster (low-growing)
Euonymus fortunei Euonymus (in variety)
Hedera helix .... English ivy
Juniperus .... Juniper (low-growing)
Vinca minor .... Dwarf periwinkle

Nooks and crannies

Alyssum saxatile .... Madwort
Arabis .... Rock cress
Armeria .... Thrift
Campanula .... Bellflower
Chamaemelum nobile ...... Chamomile
Herniaria glabra .... Rupturewort
Heuchera sanguinea .... Coralbells
Iberis sempervirens Evergreen candytuft
Lamium maculatum Spotted dead nettle
Lysimachia
  nummularia Moneywort, creeping Jenny
Mentha requienii .... Corsican mint
Sagina subulata ... Irish and Scotch moss
Sedum .... Stonecrop
Sempervivum .... Hen-and-chickens
Soleirolia soleirolii .... Baby's-tears
Thymus .... Thyme

Tolerate traffic

Arenaria balearica ... Corsican sandwort
Ajuga ....Bugleweed
Chamaemelum nobile ...... Chamomile
Duchesnea indica ..... Mock strawberry
Juniperus horizontalis
  'Blue Rug' .... 'Blue Rug' juniper
Glechoma hederacea .... Ground-ivy
Sagina subulata .. Irish and Scotch moss
Veronica repens .... Speedwell

Tolerate occasional traffic

Achillea tomentosa ...... Woolly yarrow
Arabis alpina .... Rock cress
Armeria maritima .... Common thrift
Cerastium
  tomentosum .... Snow-in-summer
Lysimachia nummularia . Creeping Jenny
Phlox subulata ....Moss pink
Potentilla .... Cinquefoil
Thymus .... Thyme
Vinca minor .... Periwinkle

Slopes

A home landscape that has a slope can be a gardening asset or a detriment, depending on what you do with it. A slope offers an added vertical dimension a flat lot doesn't have. It can be terraced and tiered to eliminate erosion, providing a creative gardener with numerous planting possibilities. Planted in a ground cover, it becomes a living backdrop for color display of inter-planted bulbs, annuals, flowering shrubs and trees. All look outstanding against a continuous curtain of green.

A slope is a difficult-to-plant area, especially if it is steep. This is where ground covers are the solution; a grass lawn or other plant material is simply ineffective.

A bare slope is more than an eyesore; it is in danger of being damaged by erosion. Rainfall and the existing run-off wash valuable topsoil away, creating unsightly and unplantable gullies. Heavy rains can even cause dangerous mudslides which may severely damage your home.

There are several ground covers that look good and also effectively protect hillsides against erosion.

The photos on these pages represent only a small portion of slope-stabilizing ground covers. For a further selection, see our land-scaping lists on page 79. Most require minimal maintenance once established. Vining ground covers like ivy are excellent as soil stabi-lizers, and their bright, shiny leaves are very attractive. Cuttings can often be planted directly onto the slope. With the heavier ground covers such as junipers, it is sometimes neces-sary to build individual terraces to hold the plants in position until they become established.

Erosion is still a threat until the ground cover has fully developed its root system and foliage to cover the bare soil. In the meantime, cover the slope with a netting (jute, available in retail nurseries) to stop the run-off. Using a sprinkler for watering will also help deter any erosion prob-lems by causing the water to fall gently on the slope.

Polygonum *is a good cover for this steep bank of poor soil. Annual morning glory (lower center) combines well.*

Cotoneaster *drapes naturally.*

This dense-growing prostrate juniper completely covers a steep slope.

Daylilies (Hemerocallis) *thickly cover an entire bank.*

Euonymus fortunei *'Colorata'*

Throughout the world, English ivy is one of the most widely used bank covers.

Lawn alternatives

If your home is landscaped like most, it has both a front and a back yard. And, like most houses, both areas are probably carpeted with grass, for good reason. Grass is the most widespread and durable plant material used to cover the ground.

But there are situations where grass will not grow, or maybe you just want something different. Ground covers can provide some attractive alternatives in such situations, and have the added advantage of requiring less maintenance. Less maintenance doesn't mean no maintenance — most ground covers need to be watered, fertilized, and trimmed on a regular basis to look their best — but not nearly as often as a lawn.

One major point should be made, however. Before planting a ground cover as a lawn alternative (or for any reason) the soil should be prepared the same as you would for a lawn. (See page 86.) After a ground cover becomes established, it is extremely difficult to improve the soil since it is completely covered with foliage. A well-prepared soil before planting will allow the ground cover to grow healthier and cover the ground much faster.

One of the most valuable traits of grass is its ability to accept traffic. That is why the backyard lawn is the usual place to bear the brunt of your family's recreation. Many ground covers will also take some traffic, although not the kind delivered by active children. But the front lawn is usually a showcase, grown and maintained for a visual rather than a functional need. Why not try a ground cover that will provide the desired carpet of green, without the maintenance that is required by a grass lawn? Ground covers even offer more than grass in a visual sense — foliage color, blossom color, and an array of foliage textures. For a list of lawn alternatives, see our landscaping lists on page 79.

Use junipers like this to reduce lawn size.

Potentilla verna *stays very low, can be walked on.*

Pachysandra — *ideal where shade is heavy.*

Woolly thyme is fragrant underfoot.

Where a lawn would usually be — easy-care junipers grow instead.

Vinca minor complements grass, grows well in shade.

Hypericum calycinum is a low maintenance alternative to a grass lawn.

The lustrous green Fragaria chiloensis.

Drape, trail, and climb

Some ground covers climb or trail as easily as they spread along the ground. These tractable plants can be encouraged to cover an old stump or drape gracefully from a window-box for a whole new look. Hall's honeysuckle, for example, can cascade luxuriantly from a patio planter and Virginia creeper can give character and color to a brick wall. Euonymus can frame a doorway and creeping jenny can creep to cover a group of rocks or the bare ground.

The idea is to look at ground covers with a discriminating eye. Instead of restricting the uses of certain plants, ask yourself what that plant will look like featured alone. What will it look like massed in a planter or pot? It is best at eye-level, or better to look up into or down upon? What you'll be considering is form, growth habit, and the vertical dimension since what grows horizontally on the ground will do some interesting things when it's made to drape, twirl, or climb.

Ivy is equally at home on a steep slope or hanging from a container. Santolina makes a striking gray-on-gray pattern tumbling over a slate wall or draped from a weathered redwood planter. Cotoneaster grows in a windowbox or creeps over a brick wall. When showcased alone in a decorative pot, rosemary can grow enthusiastically enough to cover its container.

Sometimes plant behavior takes on an interesting twist when viewed from a new angle. For instance, honeysuckle, when put in a hanging basket and left to its own devices, may twine itself into a giant green braid. Baby's-tears will ease itself over the edge of a pot and begin creeping down the sides.

The point is to ignore whatever preconceptions you may have about plants and their usual use in the landscape. If you come up with a new way to use a ground cover, try it. Ground covers will hang, trail, drape, cascade, or sprawl; they'll twine, vine, climb, creep, or spread; they'll grow up, down, over and out — just as many ways as you let them.

Muted by Santolina, *this stone wall gains character.*

Again, the adaptable English ivy: it can drape several feet.

The woody branches of cotoneaster *spill over a brick wall.*

Euonymus *grows well vertically.*

Fine-textured woolly thyme makes a touchable, fragrant mat.

Creeping Jenny demonstrates why it is often used as a nook and cranny plant.

Ground cover basics

You've decided to fill that shady corner with a ground cover, but the question is, which one? There are hundreds of ground cover possibilities. The variety in color, texture, and size is tremendous. You want something that will be attractive, but even more important, the ground cover you choose should be suitable for the particular site you want to plant. If you arbitrarily choose a plant because you like its looks, you're asking for trouble. For instance, a sun-loving plant in a shady spot will have to be nurtured and coaxed along and may never grow to your expectations. If the cultural requirements of the plant are matched with the location, you're one big step ahead.

Shade — a blessing and a problem

We've talked about shade throughout this book and there are many kinds of shade. There is partial shade, filtered shade, deep shade, and many other ways to describe different light intensities. Plants need sun for a part of the day, whether it is filtered sunlight all day or full sun in the morning or evening. Spindly, poorly growing ground covers can be revived by selective pruning of top growth.

Understand the growth habit, mature size, and water requirements of a ground cover before you plant it. It's not wrong to experiment and try different plants for different locations; ground covers are a highly adaptable group of plants. But if it's a problem-solving job you're asking a ground cover to fill, you probably want the fastest, most reliable results possible.

Use the photographs and plant descriptions in the chapter *Which ground cover?* to learn about some of the different plants available and how to grow them.

When to plant

The time to plant a ground cover varies across the country. In warm areas, ground covers can be planted almost anytime, if the water is available to see young plants through their establishment period. Generally, either a spring or fall planting is best. These are the times of least environmental stress when the shock of transplanting is most easily endured. Temperatures are moderate and rainfall is most abundant.

In cold-winter areas, spring is usually more successful. Fall plantings are most likely to suffer from "heaving" caused by alternate freezing and thawing of the soil. Young plants may be literally pushed out of the ground. With their roots exposed, they quickly die. If you must plant in fall, do it as early as possible to allow the young plants to become further established.

Where freezing soil is not a problem, a fall planting allows the plants to use the winter rains and cool temperatures to become adjusted to their new home. And when spring comes, they are already established, and begin to cover the ground more quickly. In dry-summer areas, avoid planting in midsummer, unless you're prepared to spend a lot of time watering.

Preparing the soil

Ground covers are plants that naturally grow in very close proximity, causing severe competition for space, nutrients, and water. A good soil helps overcome these adverse conditions. As a rule, soil for ground covers should be prepared as carefully as soil for a fine lawn. The advice "don't try to live with unfavorable soil" is particularly true when planting ground covers. Extra effort now most often makes the difference between success and failure.

Good soil can almost be equated with good drainage, with good reason. When water replaces the air in the soil, roots suffocate. Roots will not develop without a constant supply of oxygen and moisture and a constant removal of carbon dioxide.

A sandy soil is well drained but dries out quickly. Frequent watering eventually washes nutrients through the soil. Clay soils retain water and prevent air from getting to the roots.

The only quick way to change either a sandy soil or a heavy clay soil is through the addition of organic matter. Not just a little but lots of it. By adding organic matter — peat moss, compost, manure — clay soils are loosened up, allowing air into the soil, and they are easier to work. In light, sandy soils, organic matter holds moisture and nutrients in the root zone.

The quantity of organic matter must be large enough to physically alter the structure of the soil. "Enough" means that about one third of the final mix is organic matter. In planting terms, this would be a layer of matter spread over the soil at least 2 inches thick, worked into the soil to a depth of 6 inches.

It's not practical to go out and spade up an entire hillside and add the amendments. Besides the cost and time involved, erosion of the soil could do more harm than good. One solution is to dig a planting pocket for each plant, and fill it with amended soil. This helps the plants to get off to a good start.

Fertilizers

In addition to building up the soil with amendments, an all-purpose fertilizer should be added when preparing the planting bed. The first step in using fertilizer is understanding the label on bags and packages.

A newly planted front lawn will feature thrift (Armeria maritima). *Now is the time to pull that occasional weed.*

All commercial fertilizers are labeled by the percentages of nitrogen, phosphorus, and potassium they contain. There are many formulas, but the listings are always in the same order, with nitrogen first, phosphorus second, and potassium third. A 5-10-10, or 10-10-10 fertilizer worked into the soil before planting will get the plants off to a strong start. Spread dry fertilizers evenly over the soil (this can be done when you add the amendments) at the rate called for on the fertilizer bag or box, and work them in with a spade or rototiller. A normal amount would be 4 to 5 pounds of a 5-10-5 fertilizer per 100 square feet. Many fertilizers supply additional elements such as iron and zinc that may be lacking in the soil, some in very minute amounts. If you've had a soil test made, the analysis will help you determine which fertilizer to use and how much. If you haven't had your soil tested, a complete, all-purpose fertilizer will satisfy most plants' requirements.

The problem of weeds

Weeds can quickly overrun any planting and turn an enthusiastic gardener into a frustrated one. The most critical time is just after planting (particularly if in the spring). You'll need to keep a close eye on newly planted ground covers until they are dense enough to shade the ground and choke out weeds.

If a weed problem is severe, severe treatment may be necessary. If the area to be planted is heavily infested with perennial or hard-to-stop weeds

such as quackgrass, bermudagrass, milkweed, and bindweed, fumigate the soil after it is prepared and ready to plant. Some landscape and pest control companies offer this service or you can do it yourself. Vapam is commonly available for home gardeners and will dramatically reduce the number of weeds in your soil.

Mulches applied on a new planting will help stave off the weed population. They should be applied only after the soil has warmed in the spring. A generous quantity (3 to 5 inches thick) will stop many of the most troublesome annual weeds and make it easier to pull out the ones that do sprout. See page 88 for more on mulches.

Get in the habit of taking a walk through your garden or newly planted area once a week or so, taking a bag and weeding tool along. Dropping the weeds back on the ground will only allow them to reroot or spread seeds.

Preemergent herbicides containing Treflan or Dacthal will considerably reduce weed problems. For successful weed control using preemergent-type herbicides, read and follow directions carefully.

In established plantings, Dowpon will control grassy weeds such as bermudagrass. The label lists ground covers on which it can be safely used.

Finally, talk to your County Agent and nurseryman if you desire further information about these or other methods of weed control. They can

tell you about weeds and control methods specific to your area.

Planting

There's no hard and fast rule in estimating the number of plants for a given location. The spacing chart below is provided by American Garden Perry's, a California ground cover grower. It will give you an idea of how many plants you need. But only you as gardener-designer know the effect you want to achieve, how fast you want the effect, and, of course, your available funds. Naturally, the closer you space the plants, the faster they will completely cover the ground.

Sq. Ft. of Area Plants Will Cover

Inches between plants	64 plants	100 plants
4″	7 Sq. Ft.	11 Sq. Ft.
6″	16 Sq. Ft.	25 Sq. Ft.
8″	28 Sq. Ft.	44 Sq. Ft.
10″	45 Sq. Ft.	70 Sq. Ft.
12″	64 Sq. Ft.	100 Sq. Ft.
15″	100 Sq. Ft.	156 Sq. Ft.
18″	144 Sq. Ft.	225 Sq. Ft.
24″	256 Sq. Ft.	400 Sq. Ft.

FORMULAS — To determine area in square feet.
Circles — Area = Diameter squared x 0.7854.
Triangles — Area = ½ base x height.
Rectangles — Area = Base x height.

As a guide, plants such as English ivy, pachysandra, and periwinkle are planted on one-foot centers; cranberry cotoneaster, junipers, and euonymus on three-foot centers; trailing roses, Virginia creeper, and

A freshly planted bed of pachysandra. Note the uniform spacing between the plants.

Interplanting with annuals while a ground cover is filling in is a colorful mulch against weeds. Above, sweet alyssum combines with Algerian ivy.

other large-scale ground covers are often spaced no closer than 5 feet.

Some woody plants, such as junipers, will eventually mound up where the spreading branches come together if they are planted too closely. If you must space them close to achieve a more immediate effect, be prepared to remove some at a later time.

Spacing differs with the location. If you are planting a small area by your front door, you probably won't want to wait two years for it to fill in.

The most immediate effect (and most expensive) would be a ground cover that could be rolled out just like a sod lawn. Many ground cover plants could not be handled in this way but some, such as the often-used English ivy, can. Some growers are having success with the sod method.

In arranging the plants, some gardeners opt for staggered rows, others for straight. One advantage of staggered row planting on slopes is that it helps prevent erosion by not allowing water to run off in a straight line.

When planting on slopes it is necessary to hold the soil in place until the plants themselves can do the job. A mulch alone is sufficient in most cases. When the slope is steep, use jute or a similar netting to hold the mulch in place. Jute is usually available in rolls 4 or 6 feet wide. Unroll it from the top of the hill and hold it in place with heavy-wire staples (coat-hangers are easily adapted to this use).

Recently planted slopes, particularly ones without a mulch, are more difficult to water than a planting in a level area. There is the constant threat of erosion. Small terraces around each plant or terraces across the width of the slope can help control run-off. If erosion occurs, apply the water more slowly. One way is to use mist or fine spray sprinklers. Another method is to "cycle water" — meaning leave the sprinklers on for 10 minutes (or until water runs off) then off for 20 minutes giving the water time to soak in. Repeat this until the soil is thoroughly soaked.

Mulches

A good, weed-free mulch is a most valuable addition to a new ground cover planting. A couple of inches of mulch will keep weeds down, and make them easier to pull out if they do appear. Some of the better mulches are peat moss, well-rotted manures, ground bark, and decomposed tree leaves. There are many others of limited availability, depending upon your region. Keep in mind that materials not completely decomposed, such as sawdust or wood shavings, draw nitrogen from the soil to complete their breakdown. Avoid these as a mulch, or add additional fertilizers to compensate for the nitrogen loss.

Besides stopping weeds from growing, organic mulches improve the soil and add nutrients as they decompose. They also conserve moisture, an important consideration where summertime water is in short supply and anytime young, shallow-rooted plants are just getting started. Finally, soil temperatures are controlled evenly, creating a more favorable root environment.

You could try a living mulch of flowering annuals while the ground cover is filling in. It will hide the bare spots with color, and the annual plants will not inhibit spreading. As the ground cover matures, it eventually shades out the annual plants. (See bottom right photo, page 87.)

In harsh-winter areas, some ground covers will benefit from a mulch. With a new fall planting, a mulch applied at the time of planting will prolong the time it takes the soil to freeze, allowing the plants to become further established.

With an established ground cover, apply the mulch *after* the ground is frozen, to keep it that way. Damage occurs when the soil alternately thaws and freezes. A loosely applied mulch such as straw or peat moss over the ground cover will also insulate plants against drying winter winds. Air should be able to circulate around the foliage.

Propagation

Occasionally your bed or slope of ground cover will develop a bare spot, or you may want to extend a planting into a new area. Try some "preventive propagation" at home to fill in those

Mulching materials

Material	Remarks
Rotted manure	May contain weed seeds.
Sawdust Wood chips Wood shavings	Low in plant nutrients, decompose slowly, tend to pack down. Well-rotted material preferred. Can be fresh if nitrate of ammonia or nitrate of soda is supplemented at the rate of 1 pound per 100 sq. ft. Keep away from building foundations; may cause termites.
Peat moss	Attractive, available, but expensive for large areas. Should be kept moist at all times.
Ground corn cobs	Excellent for improving soil structure.
Pine needles	Will not mat down. Fairly durable.
Mushroom compost (spent)	This material is often available in areas where commercial mushrooms are produced. It is usually inexpensive, with a good color that blends into the landscape.
Shredded hardwood bark	Makes an excellent mulch that is easy to apply and very attractive. Lasts longer than peat moss, adds valuable organic matter to the soil.
Tree leaves (whole) Tree leaves (shredded)	Excellent source of humus. Rot rapidly, high in nutrients. Oak leaves especially valuable for azaleas, camellias, and rhododendrons.
Hay Grass clippings	Unattractive, but repeated use builds up reserve of available nutrients which lasts for years.
Straw	Same as above, but lower in nutrients although furnishes considerable potassium.
Gravel or stone chips	Limited use, but particularly good for rock garden plantings. Extremely durable, holds down weeds, but does not supply plant nutrients or humus.
Bark	Ground and packaged commercially. Especially attractive in this form. Sometimes available in rough form from pulpwood-loading sites.

inevitable bare places as soon as they occur.

The three most common methods of multiplying ground cover plants are division, cuttings, and layering. For the average gardener, division is the simplest method. All you have to do is divide clumps of established plants, spacing individual plants in the area you want them to cover (see photo below).

Gardening purists might want to extend their plants by propagating by cuttings. The gardener shown in the photo at right uses a shady, out-of-the-way spot to propagate ivy cuttings ,always having a few flats for "repairing" planting beds. Softwood cuttings are most frequently used for cutting-propagated ground covers. The terms "half-ripe" and "half-mature" mean the same as softwood. To know if a twig is at this stage, bend it. It's at the right point if it readily snaps in two.

Place the cuttings into a flat or container holding a moistened, sterile medium (potting soil, vermiculite, perlite, etc.). Hormone powders (available in retail outlets) applied on the tip of the cutting will help in rooting. A greenhouse or cold frame is the ideal location for storing the cuttings. Otherwise, find a shady, humid, sheltered area, keeping the rooting medium moist at all times.

Plants vary in how long they need to grow roots. Check them after a couple of weeks — if roots are too small or not visible yet, just tuck them back into place.

Propagation by layering is when plants form roots at joints or along stems while still attached to the mother plant. Many ground covers such as English ivy layer naturally. Spring is the best time to start layers. To layer a plant, simply tie, stake, or otherwise hold the stem you want layered down to the soil. Mound several inches of soil over the lowest point, keeping it evenly moist.

Eliminating the myth of no maintenance

Probably the best thing that could happen to ground covers is a good public relations man. He could change the image of ground covers being no-maintenance plants. Presently, a no-maintenance philosophy invades all areas of ground cover culture: the preparation of a location, watering, fertilizing, and pruning. Perhaps because ground covers are the problem solvers, (growing in areas where a lawn wouldn't be seen) they are often allotted second-class status. But ground covers are individual plants that have the same fundamental needs of any plant.

Even if you give your ground covers just half the attention you give your lawn, you'll be happily surprised at the results. There are, of course, ground covers that will grow in less than ideal soil; still others that will grow on a steep slope and won't accept anything else. But ground

covers deserve your best efforts. Given adequate care, they blanket the ground with striking color or foliage (doing the job they're supposed to do) instead of just barely covering it. Instead of merely filling a problem area, they create an area of interest.

Young plants should be given special attention. A steady watering program is very important so that root systems will fully develop. There is no rule like "water once a week in the summer" — there are too many variations. You have to watch the plants and make sure water is getting to the roots. After the plants are growing, your program should be adjusted to one of deeper and less frequent watering. This will cause the roots to go further down into the soil. Plants will then be firmly entrenched in the ground, and in a drought situation this could make the difference in the survival of your plants.

Use a sprinkler to water. Hand watering is okay in many situations but it is too easy to overestimate the time you stand there and equally easy to become satisfied when everything looks well wetted. There is no substitute for a thorough watering. If water is scarce in your area, consider a drip-irrigation system.

Check the soil for adequate moisture. To do this by hand, simply dig down to root depth and get a handful of soil. If it won't form a ball, it's most likely too dry. It's too wet if a ball is formed that doesn't easily crumble. (Soil that is sandy will crumble even

A bed of periwinkle (Vinca minor) *is extended by dividing clumps of existing plants.*

Home-propagated flats of ivy.

Mowing, trimming, pruning

You probably expected to leave your lawn mower in the garage when you planted ground covers. But there is one consolation: ground covers only need to be mowed to rejuvenate new growth, usually just once a year.

Mowing, or any method of pruning back old growth, is very important to the appearance of a ground cover. Just like watering, there is no firm schedule to abide by. When a ground cover is beginning to thatch, or the foliage loses its fresh look, it's time to clip off the old growth and start over. Generally, the best time to trim is just prior to the plant's normal growth cycle. This would be in spring for most ground covers, just as the weather begins to warm.

There are several methods of trimming, depending on the size and location of the ground cover. Bill Cunningham, a wholesale grower of ground covers in Indiana, devised the mower on stilts shown in the photograph. He reports:

"With mowing, we've reduced maintenance costs and work time, and eliminated the burden of hand pruning. Then too, mowing enhances the beauty of carpeting plants; some of the taller-growing, vining types *must* be pruned for the preferred, orderly appearance. As far as I know, none of the mower manufacturers has rigged the rotaries for clipping at, say 4″, 6″, or 8″ heights. In working this out for our program, we settled on the mower shown because the wheels were in line, simplifying the mounting of wheels on so-called stilts. We used 1″ square tubing for the additional height needed, drilling holes in the steel for adjusting for required heights. A mower equipped with a bag for collecting the clipping debris is necessary. We do know euonymus, pachysandra, *Phlox subulata,* and ajuga can be controlled in this way. I'm sure there are many other plants that benefit from mowing. We feel there is no better, faster, labor-saving way."

Weeds may appear in a ground cover after it is mowed. This happens when soil and weed seeds that have long been covered are now exposed. If you mow a ground cover so low it exposes bare soil, use a preemergent herbicide as discussed under "The problem of weeds," page 87. Check the label to see if your ground cover is tolerant of the herbicide before application.

Trimming slopes

But how do you mow an inaccessible area or a steep slope? The nylon line trimmers that have become so popular for edging and trimming can be used to some extent in trimming ground covers (see photo). Depending on the toughness of the foliage and the power of your trimmer, they can do the job where nothing else can (aside from tedious hand-shearing). Keeping the trimmer an equal distance from the ground to maintain a level cut is a little tricky, but isn't really a serious problem.

Hand trimming

Some ground covers can be improved by cutting back rather than mowing. Using pruning shears on plants such as Oregon grape *(Mahonia aquafolium)* and wintergreen *(Gaultheria* species) will help maintain compactness and desired dense growth.

An electric-powered nylon trimmer is the perfect pruning tool for inaccessible areas or on steep slopes.

Nicknamed the "Euonymus Clipping Machine," this modified lawn mower is invaluable for trimming large areas. For best results, ground covers should be trimmed just prior to new growth.

Pests and other problems

Because ground covers are such a diverse group of plants, it is difficult to categorize their pests and diseases and controls. Pests that are common to certain plants are listed with that plant's discription in the chapter, *Which ground cover?* The following are pests that attack nearly all plants, including ground covers.

Aphids come in several assorted colors and sizes to suck plant juices, stunt growth, pucker and curl leaves, cause formation of galls, deform buds and flowers, and make a nuisance of themselves around the garden. The systemic Orthene and the contact insecticide Diazinon control ahpids.

Beetles. This is a huge and diverse group of insects containing many beneficial insects as well as those that are destructive. Damage varies in almost as many ways as there are beetles. Most beetles are controlled by sprays of Sevin, Diazinon, or Malathion.

Bugs. To most people, any insect is a bug. To a gardener, "bugs" are a sub-order of insects. Lace bugs are especially fond of cotoneaster.

Orthene or Malathion insecticides are usually effective against bugs. Be sure to cover the plant thoroughly with the spray, including the leaf undersides.

Caterpillars and worms. There are hundreds of kinds of these pests. Most are larvae of moths and butterflies. All feed on foliage.

Orthene, Sevin, and the bacterial insecticide, *Bacillus thuringiensis* are effective.

Crown and root rot are fungus diseases usually caused by too much water. Junipers are very susceptible to root rot diseases wherever soil drainage is poor. Crown rot is caused by planting too deep as well as an excess of water in the soil. Roots of dead plants have a putrid sulfurous odor.

Improve drainage by grading, adding soil amendments, or planting in raised beds.

Leafhoppers are small, usually wedge-shaped insects with piercing-sucking mouthparts. They usually suck sap from leaf undersides causing loss of color and a stippled appearance on top. Orthene, Diazinon, and Malathion are good controls of these pests.

Leaf miners are larvae of several kinds of flies, midges, and moths. When eggs hatch, they feed inside, between the leaf surfaces, creating ugly blotches or serpentine trails. The holly species are frequent victims of leaf miners.

Orthene, Diazinon, and various combination sprays are good leaf miner controls.

Mealybugs. These are close relatives of scale. They may occur singly or in groups on twigs and undersides of branches, mostly in crotches. Injury occurs when large, sap sucking populations build up. Symptoms are loss of color, loss of vigor, and wilting.

Orthene, Diazinon, and dormant oil plus Malathion are effective against mealybugs.

Mites are not really insects, they are tiny spiders. They damage plants by sucking sap from lower leaf surfaces, causing the top surface of leaves to turn pale and show a stippled appearance. Under heavy infestation webs will appear.

The insecticides Malathion, Diazinon, and Orthene are effective against some mites. A dormant oil spray controls overwintering eggs of spider mites. Commonly available combination sprays that contain Kelthane are also effective.

Scale is divided into two groups, armored and soft. Armored scales live beneath an outer shell of molted skins and waxy secretions. The soft scale shell is an integral part of the scale insect, like the shell of a turtle, and though called "soft" is often as hard as armored scale. Soft scales usually secrete honeydew, causing unsightly blackening of foliage and sticky drippings on cars and walks beneath.

Except when in their "crawler" stage, scales are immobile, protected from predators and most insecticides by their shell. Scale crawlers appear just after eggs hatch, usually in the spring. To control scale crawlers, spray the plant completely with Orthene or Diazinon. In late fall and early spring, spray a combination of dormant oil and Malathion to control mature scales and their over-wintering eggs.

Snails and slugs are frequent inhabitants of ground cover plantings. If they don't damage the ground cover itself, they use it for their daytime hide-out and feed on other plants at night. Expect to find these pests wherever the ground is constantly moist — that's the prerequisite of any home for these ceatures.

Metaldehyde and Mesurol baits are commonly available and effective. Zectran spray is also a good control for the pests.

Thrips scrape and scar foliage, and feed inside buds so flowers are deformed or fail to open. They are tiny, barely visible without a magnifying glass. Look for them by shaking infested flowers into your hand or over a piece of paper.

Orthene, Diazinon, and Malathion are recommended controls.

Whiteflies. Adult whiteflies are small, pure white, wedge-shaped insects. They fly like little clouds of snow-flakes when disturbed. Whitefly nymphs do the damage — sucking juices from underside of leaves.

Orthene will control them. On some plants a dormant oil spray is effective (read the label).

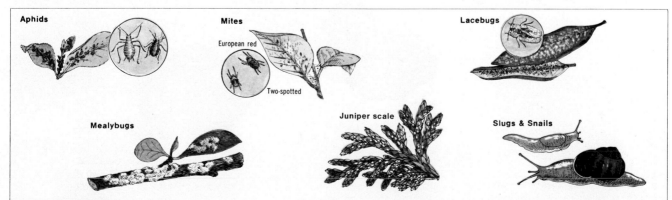

Aphids

Mites
European red
Two-spotted

Lacebugs

Mealybugs

Juniper scale

Slugs & Snails

Have fun with ground covers

Ground covers are such unobtrusive and practical plants we often fail to recognize their natural and adaptable beauty. To appreciate them beyond their obvious functional value, look carefully at their texture and form — then do something fun and different.

All too often, gardeners have a tendency to place plants in restricted, finite categories. Ground covers are obviously cover-the-ground plants, but they are capable of much, much more. Looking past a ground cover's normal use will usually bring a pleasant surprise. Thus the premise behind this chapter — to open your eyes to the many fun and creative possibilities these plants provide. All it takes is a desire to do something different.

A number of ground covers benefit from an annual trimming and in some cases the trimmings can be rooted as cuttings. This "less is more" philosophy holds true for many ground covers. Ivies, vines, and Hall's honeysuckle all propagate easily from cuttings; many succulents produce offsets which can be rooted. (See page 88 for propagation techniques.) The new starts can fill in the ground cover plantings you already have, or be potted into containers, or be tucked into a rock garden for a whole new look.

Think creatively

It's fun to put them someplace unexpected — small-leaved ivies will make handsome hanging plants indoors. Several containers staggered at different heights can provide privacy and eliminate an unattractive view. Hang some inside and some outside on the same window to create a sense of depth. Pot up honeysuckle and hang it outdoors to create a living hummingbird feeder. Make a huge topiary umbrella out of an old-fashioned clothesline with ivy (see page 96) and sit in the cool, green

◁
Ground covers do more than cover the ground. Here, a fence is transformed into a showcase of container-grown ivies.

shade. Design a fragrant spot in your yard or on your balcony with rosemary, thyme, santolina, Corsican mint, and lavender.

Let a variety of vincas tumble out of pots tucked in the drawers of an old chest or worktable. Out of doors, out of drawers, wherever — consider the plant's potential and do some alternative thinking. Ask yourself, "Where else can I use this?"

You might decide to grow a wandering Jew in the bathroom or design your house number in sempervivum.

Do a spring bouquet of periwinkle, *(Vinca minor),* and pansies. Let honeysuckle turn the gazebo into a shady, quiet place.

Consider the colors: a yellow-tipped juniper, a silver-edged thyme, a gold-dusted ivy, a white-tinged vinca, or a gray santolina. Plant the variegated

varieties in a window box and let them drape in colorful contrast with the wall. Do mixed bouquets with green ground covers trailing over the box in front, gay yellow snapdragons or red zinnias or orange marigolds behind.

Build a lath arch or trellis around your window and let honeysuckle frame your view. If you plant dwarf pyracantha or cotoneaster in the window box below the arch, the birds will come to the window for honeysuckle nectar and the bright red pyracantha berries. If your windows have wrought-iron bars, ivy in the window box will climb along the bars and give them a delicate appearance.

Think whimsically — a living checkerboard can be made of Scotch and Irish moss. Make a garden patchwork quilt combining different ground covers, or create a tiny Japanese

A lantana-shrouded mailbox provides an attractive resting spot for both letters and butterflies.

Contrasting greens of Scotch and Irish moss are a natural for a living checkerboard.

Many ground covers will thrive in containers. This juniper takes on a new form hanging from a terra cotta pot.

'Emerald Spray' cotoneaster with its winter show of berries proves to be a dramatic bonsai subject.

garden. While you're thinking Japanese, consider bonsai. Many ground covers make outstanding bonsai subjects. Combine a variegated juniper with gray fescue or use a cotoneaster with its red winter berries underplanted with moss. Because the woody ground covers, like juniper and cotoneaster, are by nature low growing and slow growing, they make exceptionally fine bonsai material.

Portable wall units can be made and planted with ground covers — herbs, succulents, or trailing varieties. Simply make a peat moss sandwich with soil as the filling (you'll need peat moss in sheets for this, not ground). Frame it with chicken wire and wood, insert the roots through the holes of the chicken wire, and water thoroughly. Once the plants are established, hang it on an outdoor wall or a balcony railing. Use small herbs for a hanging herb garden or make a collection of succulents. Do a series and cover an entire wall. Make a modular wall unit by using heavier lumber and interplanting small-leaved ivies and bright annuals. It makes for pretty, portable privacy.

Where else can I put this?

Ground covers fit into all sorts of nooks and crannies — between the cracks in garden paths, around stepping stones, in and over stone walls and fences, in any empty corner, between the exposed roots of trees, or almost any other in-between, out-of-the-way, bare little spot. One or another of the ground covers in this book will fit happily.

If you like a more formal arrangement, think about a rock garden. The contrast of rough, worn stone and the freshness of living plants is an attractive one. Find a good spot in your yard to get an idea of how large a rock garden you want. Then go rock-shopping — most builders' supply emporiums will have large, handsome specimens to choose from. Once the rocks are delivered and arranged to your liking, check to see how many pockets and spaces there are and then fill with a good, rich soil. Tamp the soil down hard — roots won't grow through air spaces — and then sit down to the delightful dilemma of choosing your plant material. Succulents are attractive and easy to grow. (See the photo, opposite.) Or, try some 'Gold Dust' ivy and some hardy ferns. *Cotoneaster dammerii* spills attractively, clinging close to the rock. Choose plants that provide some textural and color contrast with each other, and that blend well with the rocks.

There's a world of ways to go with ground covers — the only limitation is imagination. It's a lot easier if you look at a plant's potential instead of its conventional use. Ivy makes topiaries, covers slopes, and drapes from window boxes. Cotoneaster can cascade down a rock, be a bonsai, or attract birds in a window box. Just keep asking yourself, "What else can I use this for?" The answers are always surprising and fun.

Take a square-meter hike

Plants and creatures that inhabit the earth's floor are overlooked, trod upon, or forgotten. Take a bird's-eye view (as he would in a search for worms) of the ground and its busy covering, and go outside to the lawn, the ground cover patch, the herb plot, a meadow. Cut a piece of white string twelve feet long and lay it in a square. You'll become an instant naturalist.

What do you observe? How many different leaf shapes do you see? How many flowers? What creatures inhabit that small piece of ground?

Look at the tiny flowers — see how bleeding-heart blossoms got their name. Notice the delicate sweet violets, alpine geranium, blue star creeper, Scotch and Irish moss, and wild strawberry. Feel the difference between soft baby's-tears, stiff bluegrass and springy, tufted bermudagrass. Smell the earth — damp or warm — the flowers, the grass, the air. Notice color, texture, shape, and feel. Are there mushrooms, mosses, lichens, ferns? Are the fallen leaves hard and shiny or soft and furry? Are there twigs, rocks, pebbles, a mud puddle? Don't fret over the names of the things you see — just observe and enjoy.

Collector's corner

Quite a number of ground cover species have many variations in flower and leaf color and structure, making it possible for a gardener to become a ground cover collector. Vincas have pink or blue flowers with large leaves or small leaves, with plain leaves or variegated leaves. Junipers come in over one hundred varieties, and range in color from bright green to silver-blue, some with variegations of yellow or creamy white. Or, join a tradition over a century old and collect ivies. The appeal of *Hedera helix* was eloquently expressed in an 1869 issue of *Floral World and Garden Guide*. Mr. Shirley Hibberd, Esq., an English gentleman who devoted fifteen years to his collection, had this to say about ivies:

"It is not possible by any descrip-

Euonymus and tree bark in combination offer an interesting study in texture.

Baby's-tears: soft to the touch, relaxing to the eye. Think creative with this one.

Liriope muscari grows between walkway and rocks.

tion or eulogy, much less by the technical enumeration of species and varieties, to convey any adequate idea of the beauties of many kinds of garden ivies. We may be better understood when we speak of these plants as eminently deserving the attention of cultivators on account of their many varied uses.

"It is astonishing what huge, bonny, boshy (leafy) plants may be grown in comparatively small pots if they are annually top-dressed and have plenty of water from the middle of April to the end of June, to assist the growth of the season.

"The variegated kinds will prove fast and faithful friends if we will have them. All the small-leaved, silvery-tinted kinds make the neatest and brightest edging imaginable, and are as good all winter as they are all summer. These hardy, bright-leaved, pliable plants keep their beauty forever and are always improving with advancing age. The golden-leaved varieties are most valuable when the plants become large with age and densely furnished, as they are then abundantly and richly variegated and their golden leaves shine out gaily amongst the rich deep green of the general collection, making the dull winter days glad with the streaks of sunshine the summer has left behind."

Backlighted by the afternoon sun, the blossoms of bleeding heart come alive. It's easy to see how this plant got its name.

A rock garden is a perfect location to plant a collection of ground covers. Try different groups of plants for different moods to match the style of your garden. Succulents (as below), ferns, or flowering ground covers are all attractive.

Ivy topiaries— the shape of things

Topiary is the art of living sculpture, the act of giving a plant a new and amusing shape. Small-leaved ivies make excellent topiaries when they are trained over wire forms. Bend a wire coat hanger into a circle and make a Christmas wreath. Or bend some one-inch fencing or chicken wire or hardware cloth into a cone and make a miniature Christmas tree. With some pliers, some wire, and some ingenuity, you can make almost any shape.

The process itself is easy. Just take four- to six-inch cuttings of almost any ivy. Some recommended varieties are 'Hahn's,' 'Maple Queen,' 'California,' 'California Gold,' 'Gold Heart,' and 'Glacier.' Strip off the lower leaves so there's at least an inch of stem and one node to insert into the rooting medium. The new roots will grow from the nodes or eyes where leaves were. Ivy can be rooted in water, coarse sand, or a peat moss and perlite mix (use twice as much peat moss as perlite and blend thoroughly). The cuttings can be rooted in community flats or pots or simply in a glass of water. Rooting the ivy in water makes it easy to see when the roots develop; in a soil mix, wait six to eight weeks and then check the rooting progress by giving each cutting a gentle tug. If there's resistance, it's rooted.

Pot up rooted cuttings into 2″ pots, two cuttings per pot. Any good potting soil will do — amend packaged soil mixes with perlite or coarse sand, using twice as much packaged soil as sand. Wait six to eight weeks until cuttings grow about 4″ then move them to six-inch pots. Decide before you pot them on what kind of form you're going to use. For forms with a "trunk," pot six to eight cuttings in the center of the pot. For a frame that starts at the pot's rim like a cone, plant the cuttings around the edge of the pot. You'll need eight to ten cuttings for the larger shapes; the idea is to get thick, full coverage of the frame.

It will take another six to eight weeks before the runners are long enough (about 18″) to start training. Under ideal conditions it takes about six months from the time the cuttings are taken until they are ready to start training. You can shorten this period by simply buying a six-inch pot of a healthy, small-leaved ivy. Sometimes nurseries will have inexpensive

Malcolm Hale shows the differences between two of his topiaries: A 2-year-old 'Gold Heart' (left) and a 3-year-old 'California Gold.'

ivies in gallon cans, and you can repot them into a more attractive pot. If you are using a form like a cone or pyramid that starts at the rim of the pot, pinch the cuttings back two or three times to encourage branching and fullness.

Once you begin to train the ivy on the topiary frame, it will take about six to eight months to cover a 2-foot form, a year to cover a three-foot form.

You can make your own forms using wire coat hangers — they bend easily with pliers — or chicken wire. Animal topiaries can be made with chicken wire if the hollow "body" is stuffed with sphagnum moss. Pots of ivy can be concealed in the sphagnum inside the topiary.

Good care consists of watering thoroughly by plunging or with a narrow watering wand and then allowing the soil to dry out. Ideal temperatures for small-leaved ivies are 65° to 75°. They winter well indoors in cold climates. Outdoors, morning sun is best; indoors, they need bright light.

To keep your topiary neat and tidy, tuck in stray ends and trim it lightly when it gets shaggy.

Ivy topiaries are very long-lived, given good care — we know of a pair of topiary ducks that are over twenty years old and still growing in the original pots.

'Maple Queen' ivy follows a form to create a lush green wreath.

A quiet secluded place to relax is topped off by an umbrella of ivy.